ZRAC

THE
REVOLUTION'S
LAST MEN

Also by the Author

British Soldiers, American War: Voices of the American Revolution

Wenches, Wives, and Servant Girls: A Selection of Advertisements for Female Runaways in American Newspapers, 1770–1783

A British Soldier's Story: Roger Lamb's Narrative of the American Revolution

General Orders, Rhode Island: December 1776–January 1778

THE
REVOLUTION'S
LAST MEN

THE SOLDIERS
BEHIND THE
PHOTOGRAPHS

DON N. HAGIST

Illustrations by Eric Schnitzer

WESTHOLME
Yardley

Westholme Publishing, LLC
904 Edgewood Road
Yardley, Pennsylvania 19067
Visit our Web site at www.westholmepublishing.com

First Printing March 2015
10 9 8 7 6 5 4 3 2 1
ISBN: 978-1-59416-222-0
Also available as an eBook.

Printed in the United States of America.

May the images and stories of these six soldiers be a tribute to the legions for whom no images exist, and of whom no stories have survived.

Contents

Foreword

IN THE MIDST OF A LEGENDARY CONFLICT, THE REVEREND ELIAS Hillard sought the stories of the men he thought were the last veterans of the Revolutionary War. From his pulpit and in his writings he wanted people to think about wars and the men who fought them. "History lives in the persons who created it." Those words brought his mission to mind: to catalog the men who still lived as a reminder to those involved in the Civil War.

His *Last Men of the Revolution* of 1864 is a classic sought after by photographic historians and those interested in the Revolutionary War. Readers gaze on the images and read the embellished stories recalled by men considered aged in any generation. Each biographical sketch is a nineteenth-century human-interest story, as much fable as commemorative text.

Hillard's work stood unexamined until a century after publication when Hillard's grandson Archibald MacLeish, poet and Librarian of Congress, and Wendell Garrett, editor of *Antiques* magazine, took another look at the work documenting the details of the men's lives. I featured shortened versions of their life stories in my *Last Muster* series published by Kent State University Press. My work contained photographs and brief biographies of members of the Revolutionary War generation who lived into the age of photography. Now British military historian Don N. Hagist is reevaluating the sources and evidence of the wartime experiences of Hillard's men in more depth. It's long overdue.

Today, the electronic accessibility of primary source documents makes it possible to verify the facts that Hillard's *Last Men* recounted. Inaccuracies appear in the original edition, likely due in part to Hillard's romantic sense that these esteemed veterans spoke with veracity. Hillard also probably lacked access to extensive documentary proof. His mission was to capture the pensioners in words and pictures before they passed on.

Hillard trained as a minister at Yale but was also interested in local history. On May 16, 1860, he became minister at the Congregational Church in Kensington Society in Berlin, Connecticut, a post he held until 1867. Those who knew him described him as an educated and outspoken individual, a "man of fire." His passion is evident in his publication.

Hillard wrote in his introduction, "Henceforth the American Revolution will be known among men by the silent record of history alone." While we cannot hear the actual tones of their voices, their pension records, manuscript materials, and other documents are not silent. Those men speak about their lives and the world in which they resided. Generations of individuals have been moved by viewing the photographs of those last men and reading their stories.

He interviewed the men, but a pair of brothers–Nelson Augustus Moore and Roswell Augustus Moore–photographed them and published *The Last Men of the Revolution* in 1864. It was printed by H. S. Griffiths of Hartford, but the Moores held the copyright.

At the time, Mathew Brady was already famous. Perhaps the brothers were inspired by Brady's *Gallery of Illustrious Americans* published in 1850. His Washington, DC, studio was known for photographing the notable persons of his time. Presidents, theater people, and men of industry all stopped by to have their portraits taken. Many ordinary citizens did as well. Brady's book featured lithographs based on his daguerreotypes. Evolving technology made it possible for the Moores to include actual card photographs in their publication.

Nelson and Roswell Moore sought an artistic life. Nelson became passionate about painting in his late teens, and in 1850 he opened a daguerreotype studio in Hartford, Connecticut. His brother Roswell joined him in 1857 and several years later became the sole operator. They took daguerreotypes but also produced *carte de visite* albumin prints as evidenced by the images in the book. They had a thriving studio at the Allyn House, the best hotel in Hartford at the time of its construction in 1857. Nelson decided that while photography was an interesting and profitable pursuit, his passion was painting; he sold the studio in 1861 or 1862. He gave up photography to paint landscapes, an endeavor that brought him more acclaim than his photography. Roswell went into business.

The Moores photographed several different poses for each man. Auction catalogs show the *carte des visite* pictures with their imprint. The Moores also sold the images individually, for it was commonplace for booksellers and publishers to market directly to the public who collected pictures of famous people. In this period, book publishers hired engravers to turn photographs into publishable art. Yet instead of using engravings, each of Hillard and the Moores' books featured original photographs pasted to the pages.

Hillard was not content to include just images of the men. He knew that seeing someone's home further connected the viewer with the person, so he photographed the houses, hired a lithographer, and printed views of the homes "in color" in each book.

Hagist's new research adds depth to our understanding of the lives of the men Hillard sought out. This reinterpretation of these patriots' experiences proves the lasting appeal of the Revolutionary War and the value of a good story.

Maureen Taylor

Introduction

ONLY TWELVE REMAINED. Of tens of thousands of men who had fought in the American Revolution, only twelve were still receiving United States pensions in March 1864. Congress passed a resolution "tendering thanks" and "rejoicing that by the decree of Providence their lives have been protracted beyond the period allotted to man." Their annual compensation was increased "to smooth the rugged path of life in their journey to the tomb."[1] Newspapers nationwide carried reports of the resolution, bringing attention to individuals who had lived largely modest lives since

1. The resolution read: "Resolved, That the thanks of this house be, and are hereby, tendered to the gallant surviving soldiers of the Revolution, twelve in number, now on the pension rolls in the office of the Commissioner of Pensions, for their services in the revolutionary war, by which our independence was achieved and our liberty obtained; and we sincerely rejoice in the decrees of Providence which have thus far protected their lives beyond the allotted period of man, and enabled them in their declining years to receive from the government a sum of money as pensioners, which, if not as large as desired by them, will at least help to smooth the rugged path of life in their descent to the tomb.

"Resolved, That copies of this resolution, when adopted by the House, be signed by the Speaker and certified by the Clerk, and a copy of the same be furnished to each of the revolutionary pensioners mentioned in the letter of the Commissioner of Pensions, this day submitted."

Journal of the House of Representatives of the United States, March 4, 1864, Library of Congress, viewed at memory.loc.gov/ammem/amlaw/lwhj.html.

the conflict in which they served as common soldiers among legions of comrades.² Fate had brought them remarkable longevity. A confluence of technological progress and the zeal of two admirers were about to make their place in history indelible.

When a Connecticut artist named Nelson Augustus Moore learned of the surviving pensioners, he saw an opportunity. A painter by training, he had embraced the fledgling art form of photography and with his brother Roswell ran a studio for that business in Hartford.³ The Moore brothers recognized the great public

2. News of the congressional resolution of March 4 appeared in newspapers as soon as the following day. See, for example, *Boston Daily Advertiser*, March 5, 1864.

The list of pensioners reported to the House of Representatives by the Commissioner of Pensions on February 18, 1864, and appended to the March 4, 1864 resolution, read:

JAMES BARHAM, on the St. Louis, Missouri, roll, at $32 33 per annum; born in Southampton county, Virginia, May 18, 1764; age, 99 years 9 months.

JOHN GOODNOW, on the Boston, Massachusetts, roll, at $36 67 per annum; born in Sudbury, Middlesex county, Massachusetts, January 30, 1762; age, 102 years 1 1/2 month.

AMAZIAH GOODWIN, on Portland, Maine, roll, at $38 33; born in Somersworth, Strafford county, New Hampshire, February 15, 1759; age, 105 years.

WILLIAM HUTCHINGS, on Portland, Maine, roll, at $21 66; born in York, York county, Maine, (then Massachusetts,) in the year 1764.

ADAM LINK, on Cleveland, Ohio, roll, at $30 per annum; born in Washington county, Pennsylvania; age, 102 years.

BENJAMIN MILLER, on the Albany, New York, roll, at $24 54 per annum; born in Springfield, Massachusetts, April 4, 1764; age, 99 years 10 1/2 months.

ALEXANDER MARONEY, on the Albany, New York, roll, at $8 per month; born in the year 1770, enlisted at Lake George, New York; age, 94 years; enlisted by his father, as he was young.

JOHN PETTINGILL, on the Albany, New York, roll, at $50 per annum; born in Windham, Connecticut, November 30, 1766; age, 97 years 2 1/2 months.

DANIEL WALDO, on the Albany, New York, roll, at $96 per annum; born in Windham, Connecticut, September 10, 1762; age, 101 years 5 1/4 months.

SAMUEL DOWNING, (papers do not show his age,) on the Albany, New York, roll, at $80 per annum; served in the 2d New Hampshire regiment.

LEMUEL COOK, on Albany, New York, roll, at $100 per annum; no age or birth place given in papers.

JONAS GATES, on the St. Johnsbury, Vermont, roll, at $8 per month; papers mislaid.

3. For more on Nelson Augustus Moore, see Ellen Fletcher, *Nelson Augustus Moore 1824–1902* (Boston: Moore Picture Trust, 1994).

interest in the Revolution's last veterans and the value of capturing their images so that they would be memorialized by more than just increased pensions and congressional gratitude. They also knew that there was precious little time remaining for such an endeavor. They sent inquiries to every town where an old soldier resided, seeking to arrange a visit with each one. How fine would it be to offer their customers prints of their portraits! If the Moores acted quickly, they could reach them all.

In spite of having sent their inquiries almost immediately after news of the pensioners was reported,[4] the Moore brothers soon received disappointing news. Several of their subjects had already succumbed to time's relentless march; in fact, such was the latency of information within the pension system that some were no longer alive when the congressional resolution was passed. Five were gone, and no information could be found on one who lived in secessionist Missouri.[5] Nonetheless, Nelson Augustus Moore, perhaps accompanied by his brother, was able to visit and photograph six of the old veterans living in Maine, New York, and Ohio. No record has been found of the timing or sequence of these visits, but they were certainly accomplished by mid-July, quite a feat considering the planning and arduous labor involved in transporting early photographic equipment to far-flung locations. It is a testament to the Moore brothers' determination that *carte de visite* prints of the photographs were available for purchase in their Hartford studio by the second week of August 1864.[6] Their news-

4. A response they received from the pension agency in St. Johnsbury, Vermont, was dated March 19; given that the list of pensioners appeared in New England newspapers during the first week of March, the Moore brothers must have fixed on the idea of seeking out the pensioners almost immediately after hearing of them.

5. The pensioners who had died were: Jonas Gates, died January 14, 1864, aged approximately 101 years; John Goodnow, died October 14, 1863, aged 101 years, 8 months, 14 days; Amaziah Goodwin, died June 22, 1863, aged 104 years, 5 months, 7 days; Benjamin Miller, died October 22, 1863, aged 99 years, 7 months, 18 days; John Pettingill, died April 23, 1864, aged 98 years, 4 months, 1 day. The seven still living are discussed in the remainder of this book.

6. Carte de visite refers to the photographic technique used to capture a negative from which prints could be made; the prints were sized to fit onto the visiting cards that were popular during this era. The term carte de visite or cdv is applied to both the type of camera and to the visiting cards themselves.

paper advertisement proudly proclaimed: "The Last Men of the Revolution! We have visited their homes and secured likenesses of these few remaining patriots. None of them are less than 100 years old. Their 'Carte De Visites' are for sale at our Rooms, and among them will be the last survivor of the American Revolution."[7]

The pensioners caught the imagination of another Connecticut resident, Reverend Elias Brewster Hillard. Whether inspired by the newspaper reports of the pensioners or by knowledge of the Moores' efforts, he was struck with a vision. The Congregational pastor from the town of Berlin realized that these veterans were more than just the last remnants of a past generation, even more than symbols of the dogged determination that had brought about a thriving new nation. Their glorious achievement, the nation they had helped to create, was divided by a civil war that threatened to tear it apart. Perhaps these men who had served in America's first rebellion could help galvanize the spirit of those fighting to quell its second one.

Rev. Hillard determined to meet each of these old veterans, record their personal stories of the nation's birth, and hear their opinions on the conflict that now threatened it. Their accounts would enhance their photographs, giving depth to the images and allowing them to speak to their admirers. The words and pictures would become a book, a tribute, a permanent memorial so that the deeds of these patriots would be forever remembered. He would cast them as noble servants to the Revolutionary era's great leaders, the personalities that had, in the decades since the nation's founding, been elevated to mythological status. Perhaps some of the pensioners had actually met General Washington, the Father of Our Country. Perhaps they would provide a personal connection to a man so universally revered. Perhaps the current generation would listen to their venerated elders.

Rev. Hillard made his own trip to visit the veterans during the summer of 1864, proceeding west to Saratoga Springs in New York near the Hudson River, then farther into western New York before heading back east to Maine. His writings of the journey initially

7. The advertisement first appeared in the *Hartford Daily Courant* on August 11, 1864, and continued to run for the rest of the year. As will be shown, not all of the men were actually over 100 years of age.

include pastoral descriptions of the regions where each veteran lived, but there is no detailed record of the timing or specific itinerary other than the sequence of the visits. It is clear that he was in Syracuse in late July, for he found the pensioner there on his deathbed after having suffered a debilitating fall since the photographer's visit.[8] He failed to reach Ohio before the aged veteran living there died on August 15; whether he actually visited the man's home is not clear.[9] It would have been logical to complete the westward trip before venturing northeast to Maine, but the timing of his visit to the sole pensioner living in New England is not known.

We do not know whether the photographers and the writer decided to collaborate before or after their travels.[10] While the photographs were on sale to the public, Rev. Hillard wrote his text. The book *The Last Men of the Revolution* was copyrighted in 1864 with Rev. Hillard as the author and Messrs. N. A. & R. A. Moore as publishers. It was first advertised for sale by the publishers in Hartford in late January 1865, but review copies had been sent out before that.[11] The advertisement announced, "The Last Men of the Revolution.–Messrs. N. A. & R. A. Moore, photographers of this city, visited several months ago the homes of all the surviving soldiers of the revolution, and obtained their photographs from life. This collection has been embodied in a book of sixty-four pages,

8. The photographer captured Daniel Waldo in good health, but Rev. Hillard wrote of visiting Waldo some time later "as he lay upon his dying bed," having recently suffered from a fall that fatally affected his health.

9. Of Adam Link, Rev. Hillard wrote, "Since his picture was taken he . . . has passed away by death." The only direct quotation he gives from Link was spoken to the photographer "at his visit for the purpose of procuring his picture." Although Rev. Hillard does not explicitly say so, the difference in style between Link's biography and those of the other veterans, which were clearly interviews, suggests that Rev. Hillard never actually spoke with Link.

10. Some authors have indicated that Rev. Hillard was asked by the Moores to do the interviews, but we have found no evidence to confirm this. See, for example, "Last Survivors of the Revolution: In the Misty Memories of Six Centenarians Recorded in 1864, the Great War Lives Again," *American Heritage* 9, no. 3 (April 1958).

11. *Hartford Daily Courant*, January 25, 1865; letter, Edward Everett to N. A. and R. A. Moore, publishers, January 14, 1865, in *Proceedings of the Massachusetts Historical Society* 45 (October 1911–June 1912), 354.

containing historical sketches of the lives of the venerable men, with views of their homes printed in colors. The biographies are written by Rev. E. B. Hillard. It is an interesting work, and should have a large sale. The publishers advertise that they are now ready to supply copies."[12] In spite of this optimism, the book received little recognition in the press, and there is no evidence that it enjoyed "a large sale."[13]

When *The Last Men of the Revolution* was published, a reader commented that it contained "all that can be expected."[14] While intended as a generality, it is a difficult statement to justify. The men profiled in the book were pensioners, but it is clear that no attempt was made to review their pension files, the very documents that circuitously brought these men to public attention. Rev. Hillard went to extreme effort and expense to visit these men, and yet did nothing to corroborate their claims against the most obvious and easily obtainable source material. In the one case where he even mentions information from "the record of the Pension Office" he dismisses it as erroneous rather than attempting to reconcile the discrepancy between that data and what he had learned from the pensioner himself.[15] From a historian's perspective, even for a historian of a previous era this is inexcusable. But the omission can be explained, if not excused.

Rev. Hillard was motivated less by history than by patriotism. He was from a school of thought that strove not to chronicle events explicitly, but instead to personalize them and derive allegory from them. The nation, divided by civil war, needed heroes to instill a

12. *Hartford Daily Courant,* January 25, 1865.

13. A search of newspaper databases for the year 1865 revealed no mentions of the book other than the publisher's advertisement. The number of copies produced is not known; at this writing, 58 copies are listed on worldcat.org in libraries and institutions in the United States and a few others are known in private collections and dealers' offerings.

14. Edward Everett to N. A. Moore, January 14, 1865, in *Proceedings of the Massachusetts Historical Society,* 354.

15. See the chapter on Alexander Milliner; it is likely that Rev. Hillard referred to the February 18, 1864, Pension Office report rather than to the actual pension file.

THE LAST MEN
—OF THE—
REVOLUTION !

We have visited their homes and secured likenesses of these few remaining patriots. None of them are less than **100 YEARS OLD**. Their "Carte de Visites" are for sale at our Rooms, and among them will be the last survivor of the American Revolution.

We continue to **PHOTOGRAPH** for the public, and

NO ONE,

in this city,

CAN EXCEL, IF EQUAL,

the enlarged copies and finished work constantly made at this gallery .

N. A. & R. A. MOORE.

Advertisement for images of the six pensioners, *Hartford Daily Courant*, August 11, 1864.

sense of unity and national pride and also to stimulate the heroism that would be required to heal the still-bleeding nation. Washington, Jefferson, Franklin, and all the other famous demigods of the nation's founding were gone; contemporaries like Lincoln and Grant had yet to transcend the controversies and contempt that befall living men of accomplishment. But living men who had experienced the celebrated American Revolution could be lauded and feted as true symbols of a bygone glorious cause. No matter how modest their contributions, and no matter how divisive the actual revolution had been, veterans of that conflict were ideal candidates to be made perfect in the eyes of a public hungry for heroes.

With this mindset, Rev. Hillard listened to each veteran eagerly and without discernment. Indeed, he wanted to hear impressive things. Centenarians cannot be expected to relate experiences of their teen years with chronological and factual accuracy, and they were probably accustomed to aggrandizing their own stories for the benefit of rapt family members and townsfolk. We can forgive these men for elaborating, if that's what they did, and can attribute inaccuracies to weakness of memory. It is much more difficult, however, to forgive Rev. Hillard for his lack of discernment in assimilating the information he obtained. If a man professed to have been born in 1760 and yet to have been a "drummer boy" for four years during the war, that is what Rev. Hillard reported. If another mentioned being at the battle of Brandywine in 1777 but then said his first fight was at Valentine's Hill in 1781, it was duly recorded without question. If one of these aged veterans had claimed to have picked up the silver dollar that Washington threw across the Potomac and returned it to the general, Rev. Hillard probably would have relished the story. Indeed, it was accounts of Washington that Rev. Hillard sought most eagerly; that great leader had been mythologized during the nineteenth century, and by 1864 few survived who had personally met the legend. Rev. Hillard quizzed each man about personal encounters with Washington and received precious anecdotes from three of the former soldiers. He also pushed for their opinions on the present conflict and their thoughts on how the venerable leaders of the past would have regarded it. Rev. Hillard had an agenda, and historical accuracy was not a part of it.

There were additional reasons for Rev. Hillard to overlook documentary evidence. He was, apparently, determined to publish before any more of the veterans died. With the Civil War still in progress, visiting the Pension Office in Washington may have been more difficult than traveling to the far-flung but decidedly northern residences of the surviving pensioners, and correspondence would have required precious time. Most likely, though, is that it simply didn't occur to Rev. Hillard to consult the pension records. Those documents had not yet been recognized as the treasure trove of data that they are known to be today. It also bears noting that Rev. Hillard was not a historian of the American Revolution, nor a historian at all; most of his publications were tracts dealing with temperance, although he did contribute to a book on local Connecticut history.[16]

---

16. E. B. Hillard contributed a chapter to *History of Litchfield County, Connecticut* (Philadelphia: J. W. Lewis, 1881). He wrote at least five published works dealing with drunkenness and temperance, all published in the 1880s. Based on search for author E. B. Hillard, WorldCat, worldcat.org, accessed August 2014.

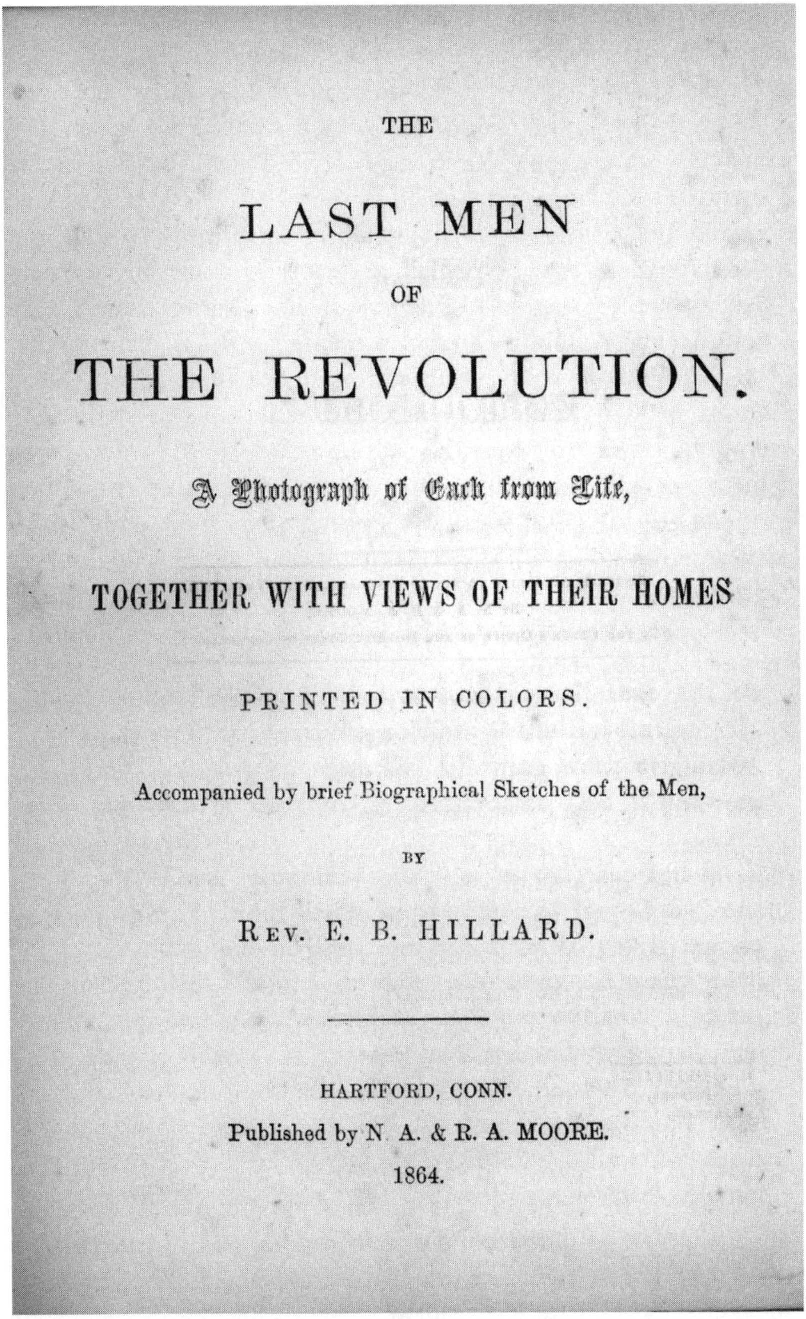

THE

LAST MEN

OF

THE REVOLUTION.

A Photograph of Each from Life,

TOGETHER WITH VIEWS OF THEIR HOMES

PRINTED IN COLORS.

Accompanied by brief Biographical Sketches of the Men,

BY

R ᴇᴠ. E. B. HILLARD.

———

HARTFORD, CONN.
Published by N. A. & R. A. MOORE.
1864.

Title page from the 1864 edition of *The Last Men of the Revolution.* (*Society of the Cincinnati*)

As a result of this, the biographies in *The Last Men of the Revolution* are long on admiration and short on facts. They are laudatory and perhaps insightful on a personal level, but confoundingly inaccurate in the history that they present. Some of the pensioners' ages are wrong; duration of service is overstated; men are presented as having participated in battles and campaigns that occurred long before they actually joined the army. In some cases the discrepancies can be explained, in other cases they seem to reflect the author's agenda of aggrandizement rather than historiography. The biographies are not presented in the rigorous format of formal interviews, but as narratives of the meeting with each man. There is no indication of how much time was spent with each veteran, nor of how the author recorded the information being related to him, although he does indicate that some men were not very lucid. In some cases passages are quoted and given in the veteran's own voice, and sometimes dialogue is used; other portions are presented as the author's recollection of the encounter. It is often not clear what information Rev. Hillard obtained directly from the man he was interviewing, and what he may have obtained from other sources, much less what those other sources might have been: relatives or neighbors of the pensioner, knowledge of the American Revolution, or his own assumptions.

Rev. Hillard wanted his subjects to be beyond reproach, infallible, on the same pedestal as Washington, loyal and flawless servants of that greatest of leaders. Perhaps he knew that some of what he heard was inaccurate, indeed impossible, but he dared not cast aspersions at the old men he revered so much. He related what he heard and put it in the context of what he wanted to hear. There was no place for skepticism in his retelling of visits with the men who'd served under the great Washington. Perhaps he fell victim to his own admiration of these men.

Rev. Hillard did a great service to history by assembling photographs and interviews with survivors of the American Revolution. It is unfortunate, however, that he made no attempt to verify the information he published and that his work was not guided by principles of historical accuracy. Even worse, the biographical material published by Rev. Hillard continues to be circulated to this day without revision and usually without question; it is as though the photographs are so captivating that they cause viewers to lose any sense of discernment and accept everything associated with them at face value, as though the textual information itself is a snapshot of actual events.[17] There have been a few attempts to elaborate on the pensioners' service, introduce data from their pension files and other sources, and reconcile some of the blatant errors,[18] but none have eclipsed the original biographies that accompanied the original photographs. The advent of the Internet has brought new popularity to the photographs and ever-wider circulation to the inaccurate biographies, as well as summaries and abstracts thereof; as of this writing there are dozens if not hundreds of web sites featuring verbatim text from *The Last Men of the Revolution* or biographical sketches based upon it.

In researching the six pensioners profiled in *The Last Men of the Revolution*, we started with the most obvious source: the pension records. These documents are held by the National Archives in Washington, DC, but fortunately have long ago been microfilmed and recently made available on the Internet.[19] It would seem that this rich lode would make short work of determining the facts of each soldier's service, but it is not that simple. The depositions, affidavits, and other material in each pension file contain the same sort of vagaries that Rev. Hillard's biographies do. Divining facts from faded recollections requires substantial sleuthing.

When the American Revolution ended, the Continental army and all its subsidiary state forces, militia, and other military organizations were disbanded. Standing armies had only recently become the norm in Europe, and in the initial stages of the American Revolution colonists had seen the British army as a tool of government tyranny and oppression. Americans wanted no such symbol of governmental force in their new republic, so there

17. See, for example, Archibald MacLeish, "Last Soldiers of the Revolution," *Life* (May 31, 1948), 88–96. MacLeish was Rev. Hillard's grandson.

18. Most notable is the 1968 reissue that includes portions of each man's pension deposition and makes use of other public records. Wendell D. Garrett, ed., *The Last Men of the Revolution* (Barre, MA: Barre Publishers, 1968).

19. The pension files were accessed through Fold3, Revolutionary War Pensions collection, fold3.com, during 2013 and 2014.

was no provision for a national army. The soldiers became civilians and returned to their nonmilitary lives, retaining no connection to the government other than citizenship. Legislation passed during the war provided a sort of pension income to some officers and to some soldiers who had been disabled, and several states offered various forms of pensions. For the most part, though, soldiers of the Revolutionary War received no reward for their service after the conflict ended.

It was not until after another international war that things changed. After much debate, an act was passed in 1818 offering pensions to men who had served in the Continental army. The act's scope was limited; it did not apply to veterans of state regiments, militias, or other organizations and was intended only for men who were destitute. Men who applied for these pensions had to prove that they had served in Continental regiments, showing discharge documents or providing credible witnesses who could attest to their service. Droves of veterans gave sworn depositions to local officials who forwarded them to the Pension Office in Washington. An 1820 revision to the Pension Act required another round of documentation to prove that they had legitimate need of government support; these depositions were added to each man's file in Washington. In 1832 a broader pension act was passed that included all men who had served in any capacity for at least six months, including those who had served in state regiments and militias, leading to more depositions.[20] This gradual broadening of eligibility for pensions corresponded to the gradual thinning of the ranks of surviving veterans as time took its toll.

Even when the first depositions were recorded in 1818, the pension applicants were giving information about service that had occurred at least forty-five years before; most veterans were in their sixties or older. While some men, with the aid of documentation, were able to give precise accounts of when they had enlisted,

20. For an overview of the process, see John C. Dann, *The Revolution Remembered: Eyewitness Accounts of the War for Independence* (Chicago: University of Chicago Press, 1980), xv–xvi; for a detailed account of the plight of veterans and the gradual acquiescence by the government to grant them pensions, see John Resch, *Suffering Soldiers: Revolutionary War Veterans, Moral Sentiment, and Political Culture in the Early Republic* (Amherst: University of Massachusetts Press, 1999).

which regiments they were in, which officers they had served under, and when they had been discharged, many others had only faint recollections of the years, durations, and names. Depositions given in the 1830s and as late as the 1850s were often even cloudier, suffering from fading memories, diminishing numbers of credible witnesses, and lost documents.

Although an incalculably valuable resource that is only beginning to reach its potential for helping understand the people of the American Revolution, the Revolutionary War Pensions are challenging to use. They are often vague, for the reasons described above. In addition, sometimes they contain contradictory information; the depositions were given in order to prove a man's service, not to corroborate every detail of it, so inconsistencies usually did not matter to the Pension Office if the basic facts of service were substantially correct. Most files contain dozens of documents, including copies of research requests made in the late 1800s and early 1900s. It can require considerable effort to sort through the documents in one file and assemble a basic biographical sketch, before even beginning to reconcile the information internally as well as with external sources. Corroborating the garbled pension information with the equally garbled biographies presented in *The Last Men of the Revolution* was no easy task, although the former is generally more reliable than the latter.

Having discerned contradictions between *The Last Men of the Revolution* and the pension files, the next documents to consult were those written during the war. Muster rolls in particular, which usually record enlistment dates and other details of service, are ideal; pay receipts, orderly books, and various other routine military documents often substantiate the times and places that a man was present in the army.[21] Only a portion of these documents survive, however, so there is no guarantee that official documents will exist for any given man. For some of the six pensioners studied here, these contemporaneous sources provide rich details, sometimes containing key information to arbitrate the vague and conflicting material recorded long after the war. The National Archives houses a substantial collection of muster rolls and pay lists

---

21. The documents, including the pension files, are cited individually.

which, like the pension files, is available online;[22] other institutions hold additional rolls and other documents. For some of the pensioners, though, not a single military document has been found, not a roll or record to prove their presence at any time during the war.

Thanks largely to the incredible searching power of the Internet and the vast quantities of period documents, from muster rolls and pension files to newspapers and genealogies, it has been possible to put together a credible biography of each soldier featured in *The Last Men of the Revolution*. Fellow researchers provided tips and sometimes direct information. Folios and fragments were found in assorted archives. For each man, it was a different source that provided crucial data and allowed a substantial and accurate story to be told; obscure interviews, forgotten newspaper accounts, incorrectly indexed muster rolls, depositions of other pensioners, and myriad other sources have yielded critical details that allow the true stories of these six remarkably long-lived veterans to be told for the first time.

The disparate information on each man—the biographies from *The Last Men of the Revolution*, the pension depositions, and the details from current research—were impossible to blend together. Instead, each chapter in this volume has been laid out as three sections: a new essay discussing the soldier's actual service and the discrepancies between that service, the pension records, and Rev. Hillard's biography; the man's own depositions from his pension file;[23] and the verbatim chapter from the 1864 edition of *The Last Men of the Revolution*. It is hoped that this will reveal the progressively changing recollections over decades as memories faded and became conflated with other accounts and perceptions.

22. Fold3, Revolutionary War Rolls, fold3.com, accessed 2013 and 2014.

23. In all cases, only the narrative rendered by the pensioner himself is included. These depositions were narrated to judges, justices of the peace, or other local officials, and the files include an assortment of affidavits and other testimony certifying the authenticity of the pension applicant's narrative. Corroborating information in the pension files is cited if it adds to the narrative given by the pensioner himself.

Each chapter features a drawing of the man as he may have looked as a young soldier. These drawings are speculative in their physical features; although based on the faces in the 1864 photographs, and using physical characteristics described in the 1780s where available, they are not intended to be "de-aged" depictions but instead are reasonable representations of what these men may have looked like during their Revolutionary War service. In cases where the clothing used by the soldier's regiment is known, it is rendered as accurately as possible using period pictures, modern research, and surviving artifacts as guidelines. The clothing used by many units in the American Revolution remains unknown, especially those of militias and irregular soldiers who may not have had uniforms at all; in these cases reasonable assumptions have been made, remaining as faithful as possible to the style and material culture of the time period.

Although photography was a recent development in 1864, it was well past the point of being a novelty. Messrs. N. A. and R. A. Moore used the modern *carte de visite* technology that had recently supplanted daguerreotype as the preeminent method of capturing photographic images. Named for the visiting-card size images they produced, *carte de visite* cameras were designed to capture several negative images on a single plate that was then used to produce unlimited quantities of albumin prints. This ability to produce prints in large numbers revolutionized photography and made images of celebrities wildly popular.[24] The Moores took several exposures of each old soldier, probably four,[25] clearly recognizable by the clothing and overall appearance of each man as being from the same session; an Internet image search will readily show most of the variations. Rather than follow the conventional practice of using lithograph copies of the images, each copy of *The Last Men of the Revolution* contains one albumin print of each man in one or another of the poses, carefully pasted in along one edge. Not only did this give each book the truest possible images, it made individual copies of the book distinctive from one another depending upon which combination of poses were used in each book.

24. Beaumont Newhall, *The History of Photography* (New York: Museum of Modern Art, 1964), 49.
25. This author has found no more than four variants for each man.

In addition to the photographs, the book also included images of each man's home. These were printed using traditional lithography; although the originals were colored, the reproductions in this volume are in black and white. These lithographs are apparently based on photographs taken by the Moores, whose studio was known for images of scenes as well as portrait photography. Nelson Moore's passion for landscape painting may have influenced this genre of his photography and the choice to include these images in the book.

In researching this volume, additional photographs of four of the veterans were found, taken by other photographers. One of the men was photographed on two other occasions. Each of these images is presented in this book, as are some of the alternative poses captured by the Moores. That some of these men were photographed more than once in their lifetimes is a testament both to the popularity of the photographic medium and to the celebrity of these veterans of the Revolutionary War.

The Last Men of the Revolution was not a significant book because it contained photographs, but because of the subjects of those photographs. Other veterans of the American Revolution had had their images captured by photography in the decades preceding the work of the Moore brothers. In compiling this book, some thought was given to including photographs and biographies of other veterans. But every book needs boundaries. Confining this work to a reexamination of the pensioners in *The Last Men of the Revolution* has allowed more detailed study of each man; it extends the original book in depth, not in breadth. Those interested in other long-lived veterans are encouraged to consult Maureen Taylor's *The Last Muster* series; it is a compilation of all known photographs of people who were alive during the American Revolution, including both soldiers and civilians.[26] The biographical information is not extensive, but the range of people presented is, consisting of over 100 images in the two volumes completed as of this writing, with more to come.

26. Maureen Taylor, *The Last Muster: Images of the Revolutionary War Generation* (Kent, OH: Kent State University Press, 2010); *The Last Muster Volume 2: Faces of the American Revolution* (Kent, OH: Kent State University Press, 2013).

Collection of visiting card prints produced by Messrs. N. A. and R. A. Moore, Hartford, CT, 1864. Notice the variations between these and the images presented in the chapter on each man. (*Library of Congress*)

Much of the text in this book is transcribed from other sources. The original pension depositions are manuscripts written in a variety of hands, some very neat and others quite scrawly. They follow no conventions of format, punctuation, capitalization, or spelling. As such, the transcriptions rendered in this book are as faithful as typographic conventions allow, with the emphasis on readability rather than exact representation of the handwritten copy. It is common for the manuscripts to have no punctuation whatsoever, relying instead on spaces, line breaks, or nothing at all to denote clause and sentence breaks; periods and commas have been added in cases where they are necessary to convey the proper meaning without obliging the reader to stop and parse run-on sentences. Capital letters are used liberally in period manuscripts, but vagaries of handwriting often make it impossible to distinguish capital from lowercase letters, especially for letters like "a" and "c"; in these cases, a fair guess has been made, bearing in mind that capitalization seldom changes the meaning or intent of the word. Spelling has been preserved to the extent that it is discernable in the manuscript handwriting. Text taken from printed sources is rendered as it appeared in the source, unless otherwise noted. Only in cases where the intended word is not obvious have editorial notes of clarification been added in square brackets or endnotes.

The information presented here is as complete as possible at this writing; just as the original volume was said to contain "all that can be expected," we hope that this volume contains "all that can be expected" by modern standards. Over time, still more details on these old soldiers will surely come to light; indeed, it is hoped that this volume will stimulate further research on these men in the countless collections that are largely untapped by researchers. There could be no better legacy than to have these six men who happened to outlive their peers be the catalysts for discovering more wonderful personal stories of Revolutionary War veterans that are waiting to resurface after centuries of obscurity. These men, connected by the chance of long lifespans and remembered because of the invention of photography, are but six of over 100,000 from many nations who served in the conflict that was the American Revolution.

In the same way that the photographs captured images of the men as they looked in 1864, and not as they looked when they were soldiers, so did their words capture events as they recalled them, not as they actually occurred. The pension depositions and passages from Rev. Hillard's visits, along with some of the other material in this book, are first-hand accounts inasmuch as they are memories from the mouths of men who experienced the American Revolution first hand. They must, however, be used with a great deal of caution, for they are tales told many decades after the actual events they recount. The men who gave these reminiscences knew the outcome of the war they'd fought in; they had experienced a modest measure of prosperity in a nation that had thrived for at least forty years when the first depositions were given, and for eighty years when Rev. Hillard met them. Thus they spoke of a common enemy and a glorious cause. The reality of their early adulthood was warfare in colonies characterized by deeply divided loyalties and stark tensions along ethnic, religious and political lines. Unification was a gradual thing that did not fully occur until years after the war; indeed, when Rev. Hillard spoke with these veterans, the nation was again divided, arguably because of compromises made during the establishment of the new government to feebly reconcile disparate values. The success of the United States in the first half of the nineteenth century had allowed the American Revolution to become remembered as an idealized victory of righteousness, with a purity that it never actually had while it was going on.

It is with appropriate historical perspective, then, that we must view statements like Samuel Downing's assertion, "Everybody was true: the tories we'd killed or driven to Canada." Neither clause in this sentence is accurate: opportunism was rampant throughout the colonies to the extent that hundreds of soldiers switched sides, often more than once, during the war;[27] and legions of men served

---

27. See, for example, Todd W. Braisted, "A Patriot-Loyalist: Playing Both Sides," *Journal of the American Revolution*, allthingsliberty.com/2014/04/a-patriot-loyalist-playing-both-sides/; and Don N. Hagist, "Would They Change Their Names?" *Journal of the American Revolution*, allthingsliberty.com/2014/07/would-they-change-their-names/.

in loyalist (Tory) regiments or resisted rebellion in other ways simply because they didn't believe that American independence was the best way to resolve the disputes between the colonies and Great Britain.[28]

Even personal anecdotes must be taken as though viewed through a clouded lens, for example, Lemuel Cook's being offered a swig from a French soldier's canteen. While the encounter probably took place, it is unlikely to have occurred exactly as described: did the teenage Connecticut farm boy understand French, did the French soldier speak in clear, vernacular English, or did the event transpire somewhat differently than Cook recounted it? This is not a criticism of Cook's reminiscence or of Rev. Hillard's recording of it, but a caution to readers that first-hand accounts are not always to be taken literally, especially when they are recollections of the distant past.

It is remarkable that Rev. Hillard happened to visit the most lucid veterans, with the most colorful stories, first. Maybe it was good fortune, but we cannot discount the possibility that the flamboyant author presented his accounts in a manner designed to be entertaining for the reader rather than a reflection of the actual chronology of his veteran-visiting tour. Geography certainly played into his itinerary, and he may have followed guidance of the photographer who'd just finished a similar tour; but knowing that he conducted his interviews with a strong agenda in mind, it's reasonable to assume that he composed his book in a sequence that complemented his mission.

Documents written when the American Revolution was in progress, depositions dictated decades later, recounted conversations with centenarians, and an eclectic array of other sources—with all the challenges of trying to reconcile this disparate informa-

---

28. For outstanding studies of the divisions within regions, see Todd W. Braisted, *Bergen County Voices from the American Revolution* (Charleston, SC: History Press, 2012) and Ken Miller, *Dangerous Guests: Enemy Captives and Revolutionary Communities during the War for Independence* (Ithaca, NY: Cornell University Press, 2014).

tion, it is important not to lose sight of its most remarkable aspect: compared to the thousands of other men who served in the conflict, we have a remarkable amount of material on these six soldiers who were in most other ways very ordinary. For the most part, we can document their military careers through the records written when they served. From their depositions and those of other pensioners we have another perspective on the same careers, revealing different details. The fading recollections of very old men bring still other aspects into focus. Where objectivity deteriorates, subjectivity takes over; facts and details give way to generalities and values. We can detect, albeit faintly, a progression of what was significant in these men's lives, what things they retold with sufficient regularity that they were indelible in mind, what things had been allowed to slip into obscurity, which tales became confused and tangled, and even the things that were embellished and elaborated upon. These are case studies in oral history, as much as they are actual histories.

Thanks to their extraordinarily long lives, the overlap of their lifespans with the invention of photography, the preservation of military pension records, and the tenacious travels of a Connecticut photographer and a pastor with a vision, we have an unusually detailed view of six men who served among legions of soldiers when they were young, and who became celebrities because they lived to be the oldest of the old. These are their pictures and their stories.

Introduction

From E. B. Hillard, *The Last Men of the Revolution* (1864)

EVERY AMERICAN DESIRES TO KNOW ALL THAT CAN BE KNOWN of the surviving soldiers of the Revolution. It was in this desire that the following work originated, and with a view to its gratification that it has been prepared.

Of these venerable and now sacred men but seven remain. Four reside in the State of New-York, one in Maine, one in Ohio, and one, if he be yet living, in Missouri. These soon must pass away. Already, with perhaps a single exception, each has outlived his century. One is in his one hundred and first year, one in his one hundred and second, two in their one hundred and third, one in his one hundred and fifth, one in his one hundred and sixth, and of one the age is not known. This their extreme age, remarkable not only in their personal history but in the modern history of the race, forbids the hope that they can continue much longer among the living. Soon they too must answer the final challenge and go to join the full ranks of those who have preceded them to the invisible world. The present is the last generation that will be connected by living link with the great period in which our national independence was achieved. Our own are the last eyes that will look on men who looked on Washington; our ears the last that will hear the living voices of those who heard his words. Henceforth the American Revolution will be known among men by the silent record of history alone. It was thus a happy thought of the artists who projected

this work to secure such memorials as they might of these last survivors of our great national conflict, before they should forever
have passed away. Indulging thus their own affectionate and grateful interest, they have done a work for which their countrymen will
thank them, and the value of which will increase with all the future.
Possible now it will soon be impossible forever, and now neglected
it would be forever regretted. What would not the modern student
of history give for the privilege of looking on the faces of men who
fought for Grecian liberty at Marathon, or stood with Leonidas at
Thermopylæ. With what interest would every lover of liberty
regard the pictures of the last Scots who were with Bruce at
Bannockburn, or of the Swiss who followed Tell, or of Cromwell's
Ironsides! How precious a collection to every true American, did it
exist, would be the portraits of the seven men who fell, on the
morning of the nineteenth of April, 1775, on Lexington Green!
Around such men there gathers the interest of the periods with
which they were associated, whose greatness they helped to
achieve. In them as the last survivors of those periods, their interest seems to culminate and they stand thenceforth as their representatives. In the memorials of such men moreover the past seems
still to live. The connection with it of their personal history gives it
reality. Ever, it is only through association with the men who were
actors in them that the periods of history seem real. History lives
only in the persons who created it. The vital words in its record are
the names of men. Thus everything of personal narrative gives reality to the past. This these memorials of the last living men of the
Revolution will do for that great period of our history. As we look
upon their faces, as we learn the story of their lives, it will live again
before us, and we shall stand as witnesses of its great actions.

The chief interest of this work lies, of course, in the pictorial
representations of the men. The artists have accompanied these
with views of their residences, that, so far as it is possible without
personal visit to them, their countrymen may see them, as, in the
closing days of their long lives, they live. The biographical sketches are designed only to gratify the natural interest which, seeing the
men, will be felt to know something of their history.

For the purpose of personal interview with them, and to procure from themselves the materials for these sketches, the writer in
the month of July visited them in their homes. It was a visit long to

be remembered by him for its interest and enjoyment, and if he shall succeed in making it to others but in part of what it was to himself, he will feel abundantly rewarded for his labor.

Samuel Downing

2nd New Hampshire Regiment

T HE FIRST VETERAN VISITED BY REV. ELIAS HILLARD LIVED UP the Hudson River valley from New York City in a town called Edinburgh, in Saratoga County. In 1864 it was a significant journey, and Hillard devoted a portion of his first chapter to discussing the region's beauty. He also found Samuel Downing to be the most verbose man that he interviewed; he was the only one who spoke at great length of his youth before joining the army. His story provides a fascinating look at a childhood experience that was not unusual in colonial America: he left his home and family at a young age to join the workforce.

Downing was born in Newburyport on the north coast of Massachusetts in late 1764, the second son of a shipwright who had served as a soldier in the French and Indian War.[1] Town records show that Samuel Downing was baptized on December 1, and we can assume that he was born shortly before that.[2] One day while his parents were away and he was outside playing with friends, a stranger approached with promises of schooling and clothing for any boy who would go with him to learn the trade of making spinning wheels. Young Samuel Downing accepted the offer and, with his new master, journeyed more than fifty miles inland to Antrim, New Hampshire, where he spent the next several years. Not clear, though, is at what age the boy left home. If Downing's account is accurate, it was before war broke out in April 1775. He said that he was "a small boy," that it was in autumn, and

---

1. Warren Robert Cochrane, *History of the Town of Antrim, New Hampshire, from its Earliest Settlement, to June 27, 1877* (Manchester, NH: Mirror Steam Printing Press, 1880), 463.

2. Downing told Rev. Hillard that he was born on November 31, 1761. His parents, however, were married in 1762 and his older brother was baptized in 1763. Evidence in his pension deposition makes it clear that he was actually born in 1764, and this correlates with him being 16 years old when he joined the army. *Vital Records of Newburyport, Massachusetts, to the End of the Year 1849* (Salem, MA: Essex Institute, 1911), 1:126.

that he stayed in his new situation for about six years before joining the army. Taken together, this evidence suggests that Downing
absconded from his family in 1774 before he turned ten years old,
although it could have been a year earlier. This was a likely age to
begin an apprenticeship, and thousands of preteen children began
their careers either with or without their parents' blessings.
Downing claimed that his parents, not knowing what had become
of their son, advertised his absence. Newspaper advertisements for
runaway servants, slaves, soldiers, apprentices, and family members
are a rich source of information about the time period, but no evidence of an advertisement for Downing has been found.[3]

The man who spirited Downing away was Thomas Aiken, the
grandson of an immigrant from Londonderry, Ireland, who was 27
years old in 1774. He had recently married and established his business in Antrim, and developed enough of a reputation for his wares
that he was known as "Spinning-wheel Thomas."[4] His new young
apprentice learned to split wood into blanks from which to shave
spokes, and to craft wooden wheels that would spin the fibers of a
growing rural colony. The outbreak of war brought the buzz of
news, rumor, and speculation into Aiken's shop. Aiken joined the
militia; he was apparently not an officer, as some histories claim,
but a private soldier in a company commanded by his brother
Captain Ninian Aiken.[5] There is no evidence that he served far
from home for any length of time, but Downing heard much talk
of the war while working in the shop and surely thirsted for
involvement as he grew older. Local men went away to join the
army, and returned with tales of campaigns. Meanwhile, in spite of
years of labor, Downing did not receive the education he had been
promised, perhaps because of the war, perhaps due to his master's
bad intentions, but maybe simply because there were few school-

3. It is possible that his parents circulated information about his disappearance
through other means than the newspapers, thus "advertising" him without leaving published evidence of it.

4. Cochrane, *History of the Town of Antrim*, 337.

5. "A Muster Roll of Captain Ninian Aikens Company in Colo Daniel Moore's
Regiment of Militia who March'd from Dearing to Ackworth for the Assistance
of the American Army at Ticonderoga on the first day of July 1777 and returned
the third day of the same month." *Rolls of the Soldiers in the Revolutionary War*, Isaac
W. Hammond, ed. (Concord, NH: Parsons B. Cogswell, 1886), 118.

ing opportunities in the rural region around Antrim and nearby Deering. By 1780 restlessness and resentment overcame Downing, now fifteen; he absconded from Antrim and made his way northeast to Hopkinton, about twenty miles distant, where he knew recruiters were seeking soldiers.

Not yet sixteen and small for his age, Samuel Downing was too young to enlist. With the war entering its sixth year, however, recruits were hard to come by. The eager lad pleaded his case and was sent on to another recruiter in nearby Hale's Town, a militia colonel named Nathanael Fifield.[6] He enlisted for the duration of the war and became a private soldier in the 2nd New Hampshire Regiment of the Continental Line. He apparently stayed in the area until this officer was ready to take him—and presumably other recruits—to the regiment, which was at that time operating in New Jersey.

Like most of the accounts recorded by Rev. Hillard, Downing's recollection of his army service is garbled and includes events in which he could not possibly have participated. He talked about the advance of a British army under General John Burgoyne and the fall of Fort Ticonderoga in July 1777, the conduct of Benedict Arnold at the battle of Bemis Heights the following October, and Burgoyne's surrender at Saratoga. Rev. Hillard interpreted this to mean that Downing participated in those events, which is impossible given what we know of his age and service record; Downing himself, however, never indicated (in the words recorded by Hillard) that he was actually in the army at this time. Everything he recounted about the 1777 campaign was likely what he heard from others, possibly during the war and certainly afterward.

There is no way to determine exactly when Downing joined Captain John Dennet's company of the 2nd New Hampshire regiment in New Jersey. He spent some time guarding baggage wagons transiting from New Hampshire into central Massachusetts, which may have been an ancillary duty on his journey southwest.

6. Present-day Weare, New Hampshire. Downing told Rev. Hillard that he went to Charlestown, which is on the western border of the state, but an affidavit in his 1818 pension deposition indicates "Hail's Town," an early name for Weare not far from Hopkinton. For Colonel Fifield, see William Little, *The History of Weare, New Hampshire 1735–1888* (Lowell, MA: S. W. Huse & Co., 1888), 118–119.

Photograph of Samuel Downing; the date and photographer are not known, but it is not one of those produced by the Moore brothers in 1864. (*Brian Mack, Fort Plain Museum*)

In August 1780 the Continental army was desperate for food and forage. With his troops on the verge of starvation and desertion rampant due to lack of basic necessities, General Washington directed a push into Bergen County, New Jersey, to scour the towns and farms for cattle and provisions.[7] The operation was called a Grand Forage, a name that had also been used for similar

7. For details of these operations refer to orders given by Washington in August and September 1780 in *The Writings of George Washington from the Original Manuscript Sources, 1745–1799*, John C. Fitzpatrick, ed. (Washington, DC: Government Printing Office, 1931–1944), 19:345–20:125.

operations in previous years. The 2nd New Hampshire Regiment was among the forces involved in the grim work of obtaining food by purchase or by force, trading deprivation of the army for deprivation of the civilian populace, paying with promissory notes that might not have any future value, plunging the war-ravaged region into greater distress and disdain of the military. By September, with the logistical crisis temporarily averted, the 2nd New Hampshire moved northeast to Constitution Island in the Hudson River by West Point. With the onset of winter they built a hut camp that was quaintly called New Hampshire Village. Here they spent the winter, wary of possible incursions from British forces in New York. When spring came in 1781, it seemed likely that an attack on New York would finally occur, the great battle that would bring the war to a close. While arrangements were being made and forces on both sides were squaring off, General Washington executed a sudden and masterful move south to entrap British forces in Virginia. Although several companies of New Hampshire troops were part of the march south, the main body of the 2nd New Hampshire Regiment remained in the Hudson Highlands, continuing to protect those posts.

Downing spoke of participating in an operation "to surprise a British train" and capturing stores and rum. His account lacks sufficient detail to correlate it with any known activity during the Grand Forage or the various small encounters that occurred in Westchester County, New York, between British and American lines. He certainly experienced some sort of encounter with the enemy, perhaps several, in 1780 and 1781. The men of the 2nd New Hampshire spent much of their time as most soldiers did, mounting guards, laboring in fatigue parties to improve fortifications and assemble huts and barracks, cutting wood, maintaining cleanliness of themselves and their surroundings. Downing talked about men being "true" in those days, apparently forgetting the punishment of deserters caught serving with the enemy, not to mention the thefts and other depredations committed by opportunistic soldiers against inhabitants.[8] He did remember the "talk about going to

8. "Orderly Book of Captain Daniel Livermore's Company, Continental Army, 1780," *Collections of the New Hampshire Historical Society* (Concord, NH: Ira C. Evans, 1889), 9:200–244.

take New York" and the posturing of American and French forces before attention turned toward Yorktown, Virginia; although he discussed the siege that encircled British forces, there is no evidence that he participated in those events in October 1781.

October brought other activities for the 2nd New Hampshire regiment. Throughout the war, the Mohawk River valley on the New York frontier was a significant theater of operations. Many of the native nations in the region had allied with the British government because of their mutual disdain of westward colonial expansion. The Mohawk provided an avenue by which British forces from the Great Lakes region could threaten American interests as far east as Albany, so a series of forts were built to protect inhabitants of the frontier and thwart incursions from the northwest. In October 1781, as British forces in the south were being squeezed, an alarm came to the Hudson Highlands of a battle near Johnstown, New York. The 1st and 2nd New Hampshire regiments were sent north and then west to bolster American forces in the area, but by the time they arrived, things had calmed down again.[9] The New Hampshire troops took up winter quarters in Schenectady and spent the next year providing troops to garrison Fort Plain (also called Fort Rensselaer), Fort Herkimer, Johnstown, and other posts.

Although this area had been a hotbed of military activity for several years, 1782 was relatively quiet. This does not mean that the troops were inactive; there was a very real threat of incursions from British-held posts in Canada, incursions that had occurred frequently during the previous years. Installations such as Fort Plain were critical to the security of the region, and were constantly being expanded and improved. Troops manning these posts conducted patrols into the countryside and along the lines of communication between posts, performed heavy labor associated with construction and maintenance of the fortifications, and also kept up the routine military activities of mounting guards and maintaining cleanliness and orderliness, and the constant labor required to keep the posts supplied with food and fuel. Rather than defending homesteaders against marauders, Downing's service at the frontier

9. Lord Sterling to Governor George Clinton, October 27, 1781, *Public Papers of George Clinton* (Albany, NY: Oliver A. Quayle, 1904), 7:447–450.

forts was probably much like it had been in the Hudson Highlands, attending to military readiness with few actual alarms. On February 27 he and other soldiers in his company received new waistcoats, socks, and shoes, garments probably sorely needed for the harsh duty and winter weather.[10] Of all he experienced during his year on the frontier, the one thing he related to Rev. Hillard was a visit to Johnson Hall, the great manor house built by famous landowner Sir William Johnson. That influential man died in 1774 and his loyalist son fled to Canada. Samuel Downing, not yet eighteen when his regiment was quartered on the estate in October 1782, claimed to have seen Sir William's ghost as he and a comrade carried illicitly procured provisions into the manor house.[11]

As winter approached, the New Hampshire troops returned to the main army now hutted in New Windsor, New York, on the west bank of the Hudson. With the war winding down, the regiments from New Hampshire were consolidated at the beginning of 1783, and again in June of that year. Samuel Downing was discharged from military service in June 1783 and made his way back to the town of Antrim where he had lived for much of his youth. He met with Thomas Aiken, and although Downing had run away from his obligation to that man he was now almost twenty years old and "too big to be punished." There were also new residents in the area: David and Susanna Downing, Samuel's parents, had moved there from Newburyport in 1781. David had also been a soldier, having served in the 2nd Massachusetts Regiment from January 1777 through December 1780.[12] Samuel's brother Daniel also moved to Antrim after ending his own army service, married, and started a farm. Samuel married Eunice George, sister of one of his fellow soldiers, Michael George; that family was also from Newburyport and resettled in Antrim. Samuel and Eunice established a farm on land adjacent to Daniel Downing's and over the

10. Orderly Book of Capt. Moses Dusten, 2nd New Hampshire Regiment, December 15, 1781–July 24, 1782. Mss. 11391, V. 2, New York State Library.

11. The dates when the 2nd New Hampshire Regiment was encamped at Johnston Hall were discerned from the regiment's muster rolls. Revolutionary War Rolls, New Hampshire.

12. Cochrane, *History of the Town of Antrim*, 463. Revolutionary War Rolls, Massachusetts. Cochrane writes that Samuel Downing met his father while in the army and served with him, but there is no evidence of this.

next eleven years they had six children, two of whom died young, all baptized at the Presbyterian church in Antrim. But apparently the farms were not so fertile. In 1794, all three Downing households packed up and left the town. Parents David and Susanna and brother Daniel moved twenty miles northwest and carved out new farms in Marlow, but soon met misfortune; both men died in 1798, the father at sixty years of age and the son at thirty-five. Daniel's one surviving child, a son, remained in the area, as did his progeny for several generations.[13] Susanna, however, carried the same penchant for longevity as her second son, surviving until 1831 when she died at the age of one hundred.

Samuel Downing set a different course, traveling to the tract of land in New York where he would spend the rest of his life. He and Eunice took their four surviving children including a daughter only four months old. They had seven more children, of whom two died as infants. Eunice died in 1846 at the age of eighty-one; Downing outlived all but his two youngest children. His 100th birthday celebration was announced in newspapers around the country (even though it was held in 1861 on what was actually his 97th birthday);[14] the notice in a New Hampshire paper caught the eye of Daniel Downing's son James, who was only four years old when he had last seen his uncle in 1794. James made the trek to New York to be part of the fete, and reported the experience to the newspaper when he returned:

> It was announced in the Sentinel of Nov. 21st, that on Saturday, the last day of November, Mr. Samuel Downing, a New Hampshire soldier of the Revolution, now a resident of Edinburg, N.Y., would celebrate his one hundredth birth day. A

13. Cochrane, *History of the Town of Antrim*, 463–464.

14. Notices appeared in the *New Hampshire Patriot and State Gazette*, November 20, 1861, the *Hartford Daily Courant*, November 27, 1861, and the Harrisburg, PA, *Weekly Patriot and Union*, November 28, 1861, among others. The notice in the *New Hampshire Patriot* read, "The one hundredth birthday of Samuel Downing, a native of New Hampshire and an old revolutionary soldier, now residing at Edinburgh, N.Y., is to be celebrated the last day of the present month by the citizens of the place in a public manner, and the old veteran is to show his smartness by felling a large tree with his own hand. He was mustered into the continental service at Exeter, and served in the war of the Revolution three years and three months."

nephew of the veteran, Mr. James Downing of Marlow, saw the notice, and started in season to attend the festivities in honor of his uncle, whose whereabouts he had lost sight of for some years past. The nephew called at our office on his return home, and gave us an interesting account of the celebration—how the soldier struggled through poverty in his early days, &c. He was born in Newburyport, Mass., and came to this state when a boy. The people of Edinburg and the neighboring towns, turned out in large numbers—and with cannon, martial music, speeches, toasts, &c., made the day merry and joyful. Among the things done was the felling by his own hands of a large hemlock tree, the planting of another tree near to his residence, and subsequently the felling by the same veteran hands of a cherry tree. The old hero stood upon the cherry tree which, with the stump and limbs, he sold at auction. The crowd eagerly seized the limbs in fragments, and carried them home, and the stump even was to be taken away, to be used as the pedestal of some towering flag staff.[15]

Grave of Samuel Downing, Clarkville cemetery, Edinburgh, New York. (*Brian Mack, Fort Plain Museum*)

Samuel Downing died on February 19, 1867. His death was reported in newspapers across the nation, which give various ages and conflicting information about whether he was the last survivor of the American Revolution, but which were all equal in their praise and admiration of this remarkably long-lived veteran.

15. *New Hampshire Sentinel*, December 12, 1861.

When Samuel Downing joined the 2nd New Hampshire Regiment in the summer of 1780, the prescribed uniform consisted of a dark blue coat with white lapels, cuffs and collar, white waistcoat and white overalls, all wool. As a new recruit, it is unlikely that Downing received any of these garments, instead probably spending his first months as a soldier in clothing he'd brought from home. New Hampshire troops were frequently destitute of clothing; in June 1780 Downing's regiment didn't even have enough shirts. In December 1781 they received captured British uniforms to make up for shortages.

Samuel Downing and his regiment spent much of 1782 at posts along the Mohawk River guarding against the very real threat of a British advance on Albany from the west. At the critical post of Fort Plain in February 1782, Downing received a new waistcoat, socks and shoes, basic items that were probably cherished by cold, tired soldiers. Here we see a young soldier contemplating his new possessions, already wearing the waistcoat, shirt collar secured by a neck cloth (stiff neck stocks were not in use by the regiment at this time), shirt sleeves rolled up. His woolen overalls extend from waist to feet and are tailored to fit snugly around the lower leg both for warmth and to keep debris out of the typical soldier's low-topped shoes. His cloth cap is representative of the many styles worn by soldiers and civilians alike for sleep, labor, or other situations not suited for a stiffened felt hat.

The regiment was inspected at Fort Plain in June 1782, when the men were reported as having clothing which had "originally been of a good kind," but was in a "filthy Condition," and "nearly worn out, which has doubtless been occasioned (in some measure) by the severity of their Service."

For more on the clothing of the 2nd New Hampshire Regiment, see Philip Katcher, *Uniforms of the Continental Army* (York, PA: George Shumway Publisher, 1981), 110-111; Marko Zlatich, *General Washington's Army* (London: Osprey, 1995), 2:18-19; and 2nd New Hampshire Regiment, Revolutionary War Rolls, National Archives and Records Administration.

Drawing by Eric H. Schnitzer

The Pension Depositions of Samuel Downing[16]

1818

[printed form with personal details written in; printed portions in italics]

State of New-York, Saratoga County.

On this *Twenty fourth* day of *April* 1818, before me the subscriber, one of the Judges of the Court of Common Pleas in and for the county of Saratoga and state of New-York, personally appears *Samuel Downing* aged *fifty-two* years, resident in the town of *Edinburgh* in the County of *Saratoga* in the said state, who being by me first duly sworn, according to law, doth, on his oath, make the following declaration, in order to obtain the provision made by the late act of Congress, entitled "An act to provide for certain persons engaged in the land and naval service of the United States in the revolutionary war:" That the said *Samuel Downing* enlisted in *the Town of Hailstown* in the state of *New Hampshire* in the company commanded by Captain *Dennick in a Regiment Commanded by Col. Reed being No. Second* of the *New Hampshire Line* that he continued to serve in the said corps, or in the service of the United States until *the month of June or July in the year Seventeen hundred Eighty three* when he was discharged from service in *the town of Newburgh* and state of *New York which Discharge is Lost and* that he is in reduced circumstances, and stands in need of the assistance of his country for support; and that he has no other evidence now in his power of his said services *Except the affidavit of Darius Smead hereunto Annexed and further saith that he Enlisted in the month of July in the year Seventeen hundred Eighty for and During the War as a private. Signd Samuel Downing*

1828

For the purpose of obtaining the benefit of an act for the relief of certain surviving officers and soldiers of the Army of the revolution appeared on the 15th of May 1828 I Samuel Downing of Edinburgh in the County of Saratoga and in the state of N. Y. do

16. Pension depositions of Samuel Downing, S. 40055, Revolutionary War Pension and Bounty Land Warrant Application Files, 1800–1900, Record Group 15; National Archives Building, Washington, DC (hereinafter cited as Revolutionary War Pensions).

hereby declare that I enlisted in the revolution for and during the war and continued in the service until its termination at which period I was a private in Captain Demick's (or Derrick's) company in the 2nd regiment of the New Hampshire line. And I also declare that I afterwards received a certificate for the reward of eighty dollars to which I was entitled under a resolve congress passed the 15th of May 1778. And I further declare that I was not on the fifteenth day of March 1828 on the pention list of the U. States.

Samuel Downing
Sworn and Subscribed this 9 day of July 1828

1855

State of New York
Saratoga County

On this thirteenth day of November A.D. one thousand eight hundred & fifty five personally appeared before me a justice of the Peace within & for the County & State aforesaid Samuel Downing aged ninety three years according to his reckoning of his age a resident of Edinburgh in said State of New York who being duly sworn according to laws declares that he is the identical Samuel Downing who was a private in the company commanded by Captain Derric whose Christian name he does not recollect in the Second Regiment of New Hampshire Infantry troops commanded by Colonel Reed whose Christian name this declarant believes was George. In the Revolutionary war or in the Army of the Revolution. That he enlisted at the town of Halistown in New Hampshire by Colonel Fifield recruiting officer in June or July but of what year he cannot state precisely but that he enlisted during the war & served to the end of the war which was about three years & was honorably discharged at Newburgh state of New York but the date thereof he cannot state exactly the year nor month, but that it was at the time that the Main Army who enlisted during the war was discharged that his discharge is lost long ago.

And the said Samuel Downing further declares upon his Oath aforesaid that he is the identical Samuel Downing described in a Pension certificate which has been for a long time & now is in his possession. That he receives the pay on said certificate regularly which has been drawn for him for seven or eight years last past by

Joseph F. Spier of Northhampton Falton County New York as his attorney & paid over to him by said Spier. That the following is a copy of said certificate.

Revolutionary Claims

Under the act Entitled an Act for the relief of certain deserving officers & soldiers of the Army of the Revolution Approved 15th May 1828

I certify that Samuel Downing of Edinburgh in the County of Saratoga in the State of New York is entitled to receive pay under the above mentioned act as a surviving private of infantry in the New Hampshire line of the Army of the Revolution at the rate of six dollars & sixty six 2/3 cents a month payable during his life on the third day of March & third day of September in each year.

It is provided by law that the said pay shall not in any way be transferable or liable to attachment, levy or seizure by any legal process whatever.

Given under my hand & the seal of the Treasury of the United States this third day of August in the year one thousand eight hundred & twenty nine & of Independence fifty fourth.

T. D. Ingham, Secretary of the Treasury

He makes this declaration for the purpose of obtaining the bounty land to which he may be entitled under the act approved March 3d 1855. He also declares that he has not received a warrant for bounty land under this or any other act of congress, nor made any other application thereof to his knowledge or recollection. But that he has been informed that it appears from the records in some office at Washington that one hundred acres or some other quantity of land has been drawn on his account but that he had no recollection of making any application thereof or of authorizing any person to make such application & has no other knowledge or information that any such bounty land has been obtained as aforesaid except from what he has been informed as aforesaid but that he cannot say positively that no bounty land has been obtained as aforesaid by his authority & that in case it appears that any such bounty lands has been duly obtained on his account then this declaration is made for the purpose of obtaining the additional bounty land to which he may be entitled under said act.

Samuel Downing.

RESIDENCE of SAMUEL DOWNING.

LITH. OF BINGHAM & DODD, HARTFORD, CT.

Lithograph of Samuel Downing's home, Summer 1864, from *Last Men of the Revolution*. (*Society of the Cincinnati*)

Samuel Downing

From E. B. Hillard, The Last Men of the Revolution (1864)

THE FIRST IN ORDER VISITED WAS SAMUEL DOWNING, AND THE sketch of his life shall introduce the series.

Mr. Downing lives in the town of Edinburgh, Saratoga County, New York. His age is one hundred and two years. To reach his home, you proceed to Saratoga, and thence by stage some twenty miles to the village of Luzerne, on the upper Hudson. Here you are at once rewarded for your journey thus far. Few spots more beautiful are to be found. The river, flowing above it broad and free, at this point is compressed within a narrow gorge some twelve or fifteen feet in width, through which, after passing over a series of rapids known as Rockwells Falls, it rushes with great rapidity and force, the sound of its waters filling the air with music and your heart with freshness as you listen to them, ceaseless, by day or by night. Around the village tower the mountains of the region, southern spurs of the Adirondacks; one, a solitary, lofty dome, a landmark far and wide. But the gem of the village seemed to me its lake. This lies a little out of and above it, and for completeness and exquisiteness of beauty is not unworthy the vicinity of Lake George, from the head of which, connected with it by a series of lesser lakes, it is distant but twelve miles. I viewed it by moonlight on the evening of my arrival. The night was still, and the smoky haze that brooded over all the region subdued and softened the outlines of the mountain masses which are its setting. And there, in their mingled shadow and the moonlight, lay the lake, the forests fringing it to its very edge, its shores winding in and out among them, a beautiful wooded island rising from its centre, with the dip of oars and the voices of singers from parties of evening voyagers coming sweetly to the land, together forming a scene which for soft and dreamlike effect seemed more befitting the style of Italy than the stern and rugged scenery of our northern America. Add to this the attraction of a pleasant hotel within near sight and sound of the river rapids, with one of the cheeriest and most obliging of landlords, and it is not strange that Luzerne should be adopted, as it is, as a place of summer resort by many families of wealth and leisure from the cities below.

From Luzerne the home of Mr. Downing is distant some twenty-five miles up the valley of the Sacandaga river, and for it I set out early on the following morning. The Sacandaga is a branch of the Hudson, putting into it from the west just below Luzerne. Its valley is narrow and walled in on both sides by high mountains; those on the southern side, known as the Kayderasseras (the title of an early patent) or Greenfield Mountains, separating it from the valley of the Mohawk. It was through this valley that Sir John Johnson, in 1780, made his incursion from Canada by way of Crown Point into the Mohawk valley, and by the head of it and the Indian paths west of the Adirondack Mountains that he returned. Near the head of the valley the river makes a broad bend to the southwest round a point of hills, coming up on their western side to Lake Pleasant, its source. At the head of this bend, about midway between the lake and the river, upon the summit of the intervening highlands, stands the house of Mr. Downing, built by himself, the first framed house in the town of Edinburgh, seventy years ago. It was about noon when I reached there; and as I drove up I observed on the eastern side of the house, near the front corner of it, (the corner nearest you in the picture,) seated between two bee-hives, bending over, leaning upon his cane and looking on the ground, an old man, whom I at once concluded to be the object of my search. Indeed, once in the vicinity you have no difficulty in finding him, as all in the region know "Old Father Downing," and speak of him with respect and affection. The celebration of his one hundredth birthday, to which the whole country around gathered, served to make him acquainted with many who might otherwise, in the seclusion of his age, have lost sight of him. On entering the yard I at once recognized him from his photograph,[17] and addressing myself to him, said, "Well, Mr. Downing, you and the bees

17. This statement makes it clear that Rev. Hillard had already seen the photographs of Downing produced by the Moore brothers.

seem very good friends." (There was barely room for him between the two hives, and the swarms were working busily on both sides of him.) "Yes," he replied, "they don't hurt me and I don't hurt them." On telling him that I had come a long way to see an old soldier of the Revolution, he invited me to walk into the house, himself leading the way. The day was extremely warm. I inquired of him which suited him best, warm weather or cold. "If I had my way about it" he answered, "I should like it about so. But we can't do that: we have to take it as it comes." The day before had been one of the hottest of the season, so much so that coming up by stage from Saratoga, we could scarcely endure the journey. Yet in the middle of it, the old man, they told me, walked some two miles and a half over a very tedious road to the shoemaker's, got his boots tapped,[18] and walked home again. Mr. Downing is altogether the most vigorous in body and mind of the survivors. Indeed, judging from his bearing and conversation, you would not take him to be over seventy years of age. His eye is indeed dim, but all his other faculties are unimpaired, and his natural force is not at all abated. Still he is strong, hearty, enthusiastic, cheery: the most sociable of men and the very best of company. He eats his full meal, rests well at night, labors upon the farm, "hoes corn and potatoes, and works just as well as anybody." His voice is strong and clear, his mind unclouded, and he seems, as one of his neighbors said of him, "as good for ten years longer as he ever was." Seated in the house, and my errand made known to him, he entered upon the story of his life, which I will give as nearly as possible in the old man's own words.

"I was born," said he, "in the town of Newburyport, Mass., on the 31st of November, 1761.[19] One day, when I was a small boy, my parents went across the bay in a sail-boat to a place called Joppa. They left me at home; and I went out into the street to play marbles with the boys.[20] As we were playing, a man came along and asked if we knew of any boy who would like to go and learn the trade of spinning-wheel making. Nobody answered; so I spoke up, and said, 'Yes, I want to go.' 'Where are your parents?' asked he. 'They ain't at home,' said I; 'but that won't make no odds; I will go.'

18. Boots tapped, that is, having reinforcements put on the soles and heels.
19. As described above, Downing was born in 1764.
20. As described above, this probably occurred in 1774.

So he told me that if I would meet him that afternoon at Greenleaf's tavern, (I remember the tavern keeper's name,) he would take me. So I did. They asked me at the tavern where I was going. I told them I was going off. So we started; he carried me to Haverhill, and the next day to Londonderry, where we stayed over Sunday. It was the fall of the year. I remember the fruit was on the ground, and I went out and gathered it. I was happy yet. From Londonderry he carried me to Antrim, where he lived. His name was Thomas Aiken. Antrim was a wooded country then. When I got there I was homesick; so I went into the woods and sat down on a hemlock log, and cried it out. I was sorry enough I had come. When I went back to the house they accused me of it; but I denied it. I staid with Mr. Aiken till after the breaking out of the war, working at wheels during the day and splitting out spokes at night. I had lived with him so six years. He didn't do by me as he agreed to. He agreed to give me so much education, and at the end of my time an outfit of clothes, or the like, and a kit of tools. So I tells aunt, (I used to call Mr. Aiken uncle and his wife aunt,) 'Aunty, Uncle don't do by me as he agreed to. He agreed to send me to school, and he hasn't sent me a day;' and I threatened to run away. She told if I did they'd handcuff me and give me a whipping. 'But,' said I, 'You'll catch me first, won't you, Aunty?' 'O,' she said, 'they'd advertise me.'[21]

"Well, the war broke out. Mr. Aiken was a militia captain; and they used to be in his shop talking about it. I had ears, and I had *eyes* in them days. They was enlisting three years men and for-the-war men.[22] I heard say that Hopkinton was the enlisting place. One day aunt said she was going a-visiting. So I said to myself, 'That's right, Aunty; you go, and I'll go too.' So they went out, and I waited till dinner time, when I thought nobody would see me, and then I started. I had a few coppers, but I darsn't take any of my clothes, for fear they'd have me up for a thief. It was eighteen miles, and I went it pretty quick. The recruiting officer, when I told him what I'd come for, said I was too small. I told him just what I'd done. 'Well,' said he, 'you stay here and I'll give you a letter to Col. Fifield over in Charlestown and perhaps he'll take you.' So I staid with

21. Advertise, that is, they would circulate notices by word of mouth, hand-bills, or in newspapers.

22. For-the-war men, that is, men who enlisted for the duration of the war rather than for a specific term of service.

him; and when uncle and aunt came home that night they had no Sam. The next day I went and carried the letter to Col. Fifield, and he accepted me. But he wasn't quite ready to go: he had his haying to do; so I staid with him and helped him through it, and then I started for the war. Uncle spent six weeks in looking for me, but he didn't find me."

"But did your parents hear nothing of you all this time?"

"Yes; Mr. Aiken wrote to them about a year after he stole me. They had advertised me and searched for me, but at last concluded I had fallen off the dock and been drowned.

"The first duty I ever did was to guard wagons from Exeter to Springfield. We played the British a trick; I can remember what I said as well as can be. We all started off on a run, and as I couldn't see anything, I said, 'I don't see what the devil we're running after or running away from; for I can't see anything.' One of the officers behind me said, 'Run, you little dog, or I'll spontoon you.'[23] 'Well,' I answered, 'I guess I can run as fast as you can and as far.' Pretty soon I found they were going to surprise a British train. We captured it; and among the stores were some hogsheads of rum. So when we got back to camp that night the officers had a great time drinking and gambling; but none for the poor soldiers. Says one of the sergeants to me, 'We'll have some of that rum.' It fell to my lot to be on sentry that night; so I couldn't let 'em in at the door. But they waited till the officers got boozy; then they went in at the windows and drew a pailful, and brought it out and we filled our canteens, and then they went in and drew another. So we had some of the rum; all we wanted was to live with the officers, not any better.

"Afterwards we were stationed in the Mohawk Valley. Arnold was our fighting general, and a bloody fellow he was.[24] He didn't

<hr>

23. Spontoon, or espontoon, a spear-like bladed weapon on a long pole carried by officers; it could be used for personal defense, but was primarily so that the officer could be readily identified from a distance by his men.

24. As discussed above, Downing's regiment went to the Mohawk Valley in late 1781. Benedict Arnold had gone over to the British side in late 1780, shortly after Downing joined the army; it is possible that, on his journey from New Hampshire to join his regiment, Downing saw Arnold in the Hudson Highlands, but this is only speculation. More likely Downing recalled what he'd learned about Arnold from others during and after the war.

care for nothing; he'd ride right in. It was 'Come on, boys!' 'twasn't 'Go, boys!' He was as brave a man as ever lived. He was dark-skinned, with black hair, of middling height. There wasn't any waste timber in him. He was a stern looking man, but kind to his soldiers. They didn't treat him right: he ought to have had Burgoyne's sword.[25] But he ought to have been true. We had true men then; 'twasn't as it is now. Everybody was true: the tories we'd killed or driven to Canada."

"You don't believe, then, in letting men stay at their homes and help the enemy?"

"Not by a grand sight!" was his emphatic reply. "The men that caught Andre were true. He wanted to get away, offered them everything. Washington hated to hang him; he cried, they said."[26]

The student of American history will remember the important part which Arnold performed in the battle connected with the surrender of Burgoyne. Mr. Downing was engaged.[27]

"We heard," he said, "Burgoyne was coming. The tories began to feel triumphant. One of them came in one morning and said to his wife, 'Ty (Ticonderoga) is taken, my dear.' But they soon changed their tune. The first day at Bemis Heights both claimed the victory. But by and by we got Burgoyne where we wanted him, and he gave up. He saw there was no use in fighting it out. There's where I call 'em *gentlemen*. Bless your body, we had *gentlemen* to fight with in those days. When they was whipped they gave up. It isn't so now.

"Gates was an 'old granny' looking fellow. When Burgoyne came up to surrender his sword, he said to Gates, 'Are you a general? You look more like a granny than you do like a general.' 'I be

25. He ought to have had Burgoyne's sword, that is, Downing felt that when General Burgoyne handed over his sword in the ceremonial gesture of surrender, Benedict Arnold should have received it rather than Horatio Gates.

26. Downing refers to the capture of British Major John André in October 1780. André was carrying messages from Benedict Arnold when he was stopped by three American militiamen; André tried to gain freedom by bribing his captors, but they refused. André's capture revealed Benedict Arnold's treason.

27. As discussed above, Downing was not in the army in 1777; Downing does not say that he was, but Rev. Hillard seems to have inferred it.

a granny,' said Gates, 'and I've delivered you of ten thousand men to-day.'[28]

"Once, in the Mohawk valley, we stopped in William Johnson's great house.[29] It would hold a regiment. Old Johnson appeared to us: I don't know as you'll believe it. The rest had been out foraging. One had stolen a hive of honey; some others had brought in eight quarters of good mutton, and others, apples and garden sauce,[30] and so forth. Ellis[31] and I went out to get a sack of potatoes, some three pecks. When we got back to Johnson's, as we were going through the hall, I looked back, and there was a man. I can see now just how he looked. He had on a short coat. What to do with the potatoes we didn't know. It wouldn't do to carry them into the house; so I ran down cellar. When the man got to the middle of the hall, all at once he disappeared. I could see him as plain—O, if I could see you as plain![32]

"By and by they began to talk about going to take New York. There's always policy, you know, in war. We made the British think we were coming to take the city. We drew up in line of battle: the British drew up over there, (pointing with his hand.) They looked very handsome. But Washington went south to Yorktown. La Fayette laid down the white sticks, and we threw up entrenchments by them.[33] We were right opposite Washington's headquarters. I saw him every day."[34]

---

28. Although the nickname "Granny Gates" is widely believed to have been used during the American Revolution, the first published mention of it appears in an 1823 novel by John Neal, *Seventy-Six: Our Country, Right or Wrong* (Baltimore: Joseph Robinson, 1828); it was released in England in 1840 as *Seventy-Six: Love and War*.

29. Johnson Hall, Johnstown, New York.

30. Garden sauce, that is, greens to complement a meal of meat and potatoes.

31. Robert Ellis was about the same age as Downing (he gave his age as 52 in 1818, just as Downing did), enlisted at about the same time, and served in the same company of the 2nd New Hampshire regiment. Their names are next to each other on many of the muster rolls. He settled in Maine after the war and died on November 25, 1846. Pension deposition of Robert Ellis, W. 23005, Revolutionary War Pensions.

32. As discussed above, Sir William Johnson died on July 11, 1774. Downing again makes light of his failing eyesight.

33. Laid down the white sticks, that is, marked out the locations of encampments or entrenchments.

34. Here Downing probably refers to the cantonment at New Windsor, New York, in late 1782 and early 1783; there is no evidence that Downing was on the campaign to Yorktown.

"Was he as fine a looking man as he is reported to have been?"

"Oh!" he exclaimed, lifting up both his hands and pausing, "but you never got a smile out of him. He was a nice man. We loved him. They'd sell their lives for him." I asked, "What do you think he would say if he was here now?"

"Say!" exclaimed he, "I don't know, but he'd be mad to see me sitting here. I tell 'em if they'll give me a horse I'll go as it is. If the rebels come here, I shall sartingly take my gun.[35] I can see best furtherest off."

"How would Washington treat traitors if he caught them?"

"Hang 'em to the first tree!" was his reply.

He denounces the present rebellion, and says he only wishes to live to see it crushed out. His father and his wife's father were in the French War. His brother was out through the whole war of the Revolution. He has a grandson now in the army, an officer in the Department of the Gulf,—a noble looking young man, as represented by his photograph. He has been in the service from the beginning of the war.

"When peace was declared," said the old man, concluding his story of the war, "we burnt thirteen candles in every hut, one for each State."[36]

I have given his narrative in his own words, because to me, as I listened, there was an unequaled charm in the story of the Revolution, broken and imperfect though it was, from the lips of one who was a living actor in it. The very quaintness and homeliness of his speech but added to the impression of reality and genuineness. I felt as I listened to him that the story which he told was true.

At the close of the war, Mr. Downing returned to Antrim, "too big," as he said, "for Aunty to whip." Soon after his return, he married Eunice George, aged eighteen years. She died eleven years ago. By her he had thirteen children. Three of these are now living. The one with whom he resides is his youngest son, and, though himself seventy-three years old, his father addresses him still as "Bub." He came from Antrim to Edinburgh in 1794, "And to

35. "Sartingly," that is, "certainly."

36. The peace treaty was declared on November 30, 1782, and it took some time for word to reach the cantonments where American soldiers typically spent winters in huts.

show you," said he, "that there was one place I didn't run away from, I will give you this," handing me the following certificate

> To All Whom It May Concern.
>
> This may certify that the bearer, Samuel Downing, with his wife, have been good members of society; has received the ordinance of baptism for their children in our church; and is recommended to any church or society, where Providence is pleased to fix them, as persons of good moral character. Done in behalf of the Session.
>
> Isaac Coshran, Session Clerk.
> *Antrim, Feb. 27, 1794.*

"It must have been a pretty wild country when you came here?"

"O, there wasn't a marked tree; it was all a wilderness."

"How came you to come?"[37]

"They said in Antrim we could live on three days' work here as easy as we could on six there. So we formed a company to come. There were some twenty, but I was the only one that came. I sold my farm there, one hundred and ten acres, for a trifle; and my brother and I came out here to look. As soon as we got here and saw the country, I said to my brother, 'I've given my farm away, and have nothing to buy another with: so I've got to stay here. But you've sold well: so you go right back and buy another.' All the land round here was owned by old Domine Gross.[38] I took mine of a Mr. Foster; and when I'd chopped ten acres and cleared it and fenced it, I found my title wasn't good: that Mr. Foster hadn't fulfilled the conditions on which he had it of Mr. Gross. So we went down together to see the Domine about it. I told him I'd paid for the land. 'No matter,' said he, 'it isn't yours.' 'But,' said I, 'Mr. Gross, I've chopped ten acres and cleared it and fenced it; aint I to have anything for my labor?' 'I don't thank you,' he replied, 'for cutting my timber.' Then I began to be scared. So says I, 'Mr. Foster, I guess we'd better be getting along towards home.' 'O, you can have the land,' says the old Domine, 'only you must give me fifty pounds more; and you can make me a little sugar now and then.' 'Well,' said I, 'I will go over to your agent and get the papers.' 'O, I can do the writing,' said he. So I paid the money and got the land."

37. That is, it was much easier to make a living in Saratoga County than in Antrim.

38. "Domine," a lord or master.

And on it he has lived and labored for seventy years. Its neighborhood to his old battle-grounds might have had its influence in determining his selection of it for a home.

At the age of one hundred, Mr. Downing had never worn glasses, or used a cane. The fall before, he had pulled, trimmed, and deposited in the cellar, in one day, fifteen bushels of carrots. His one hundredth birthday was celebrated by his neighbors and friends, upon his farm, with a large concourse, estimated at a thousand persons, the firing of one hundred guns, and an address by George S. Batcheller, Esq., of Saratoga.[39] On this occasion the old man cut down a hemlock tree five feet in circumference, and later in the day a wild cherry tree near his house, of half this size.[40] He says he could do it again, and it is likely that he could. The trees were sold upon the ground, and stripped of their branches by those present for canes and other mementoes of the occasion. The stump of the larger one was sawed off and carried to Saratoga by Robert Bevins, of that place. The axe with which the trees were cut was sold for seven dollars and a half.

Mr. Downing lives very comfortably with his son, James M. Downing. His health has always been good. His pension, formerly eighty dollars a year, was increased at the last session of Congress to one hundred and eighty dollars. He pays no particular attention to his diet; drinks tea and coffee, and smokes tobacco. He gets tired sometimes, his son says, during the day; but his sleep at night restores him like a child. It is a curious circumstance that his hair, which until lately has been for many years silvery white, is now beginning to turn black. In a lock of it, lying before me as I write, there are numerous perfectly black hairs.

By religious persuasion, Mr. Downing is a Methodist. "Why," said he, "I'll tell you: because they are opposed to slavery, and believe in a free salvation."

He is as staunch in his religious belief as he is in his personal character; expounds his faith intelligently and forcibly; believes thoroughly what he believes, and rejects earnestly what he rejects.

39. George Sherman Batcheller, a prominent Saratoga lawyer and officer in the Union army.

40. An obituary repeated this story that "Mr. Downing cut down a hemlock tree 22 inches in diameter, a black cherry tree measuring a foot in diameter" but added, "and then digging a hole through the snow and frost, planted a small tree." *New England Historical and Genealogical Register* 21:3 (July 1867), 288.

Among the latter is the doctrine of reprobation, concerning which he tells the story of a controversy which he had with an old Methodist preacher, who held and preached the doctrine.[41]

"'You believe,' said he, 'that God from eternity has elected a part and reprobated a part of mankind?' 'Yes,' replied the preacher, 'that is my belief.' 'Have you wicked children?' 'Yes.' 'Do you pray for them?' 'Yes.' 'Have you wicked neighbors?' 'Yes.' 'Do you pray for them?' 'Yes.' 'But how do you know but they are reprobated?' He didn't say anything in reply then. A while after I met him, and asked him if he still believed in reprobation. 'No,' he answered, 'I've thrown away that foolish notion.'"

Mr. Downing's faith in the Invisible is firm and clear, and his anticipation of the rest and reward of Heaven strong and animating. He greatly enjoys religious conversation, invokes a blessing at the table; and when prayer was offered, at his request, responded intelligently and heartily, in true Methodist style. Doubtless, when the earthly house of this tabernacle is dissolved, he will find awaiting him "a building of God, an house not made with hands, eternal in the heavens."[42]

The sun was drawing low as I left him, to return to Luzerne. My interview with him had been most interesting and delightful. I parted from him with regret. His eyes filled with tears as, in bidding him good-bye, I mentioned that better country where I should hope again to meet him. As I rode away, I turned my eyes southward over the valley of the Mohawk, bounded in the dim distance by the Catskill Mountains. I felt anew how great the change which a hundred years has wrought, which a single lifetime covers. I had just parted from a man still living who had hunted the savage through that valley now thronged with cities and villages–in place of the then almost unbroken wilderness, now fair fields and pleasant dwellings–in place of constant peril and mortal conflict, now security and peace; and my heart swelled afresh with gratitude to the men who had rescued their land from the tyrant and the savage, and had made it for their children so fair and happy a home.

41. Reprobation, the belief that some are excluded by God from salvation.
42. Rev. Hillard quotes 2 Corinthians 5:1.

Samuel Downing, photographed by Messrs. N. A. and R. A. Moore, 1864. (*Society of the Cincinnati*)

Daniel Waldo

Connecticut Militia

ONE OF THE AGED SOLDIERS VISITED BY REV. HILLARD HAD achieved a modest level of celebrity in his later years, due in part to his status as a Revolutionary War veteran and in part to his postwar career in the church. Daniel Waldo spent most of his life in Connecticut before resettling in New York at the age of 72. His achievements as a soldier were modest by any standard, and it was his work as a clergyman that brought him social status and a life of reasonable comfort. He was, nonetheless, a war veteran who had experienced some significant military adventures and hardships before his twentieth year. The few recollections recorded by Rev. Hillard that were related secondhand because of Waldo's sudden decline in health, and Waldo's own pension deposition, present his military career so briefly that it seems almost like a casual aside in his life, like a year of study at a discarded avocation or a failed business venture. His account of being captured says nothing of fellow soldiers being brutally slain by sabers only yards away from him; his mention of having been a prisoner of war omits that hundreds of others perished in the same prison; only through the depositions of comrades do we learn of overnight marches without food. Fortunately we can assemble a more detailed account of his service through the narratives of other soldiers who served alongside him.

Considering his age, it is surprising that Daniel Waldo saw as little military service as he did. He was born in Windham, Connecticut, in 1762, and we have no information about his early life other than his parentage and the presumption that it was unremarkable. He came of age at a time when war raged in New England. His home colony was flanked by British garrisons in New York and Rhode Island, and ships from both sides plied Connecticut's coastal waters. How this young man managed to serve for just eleven months (only nine of which he'd planned on) is not explained by him. Connecticut militia law, established in 1758, did not specify a minimum age for military service but stipulated only that "all able-bodied men" up to the age of 45 serve.[1] Waldo turned 16 in September 1778, and was drafted into the militia the following April.

He served for one month in a company commanded by Capt. William Howard, and his activity was more that of the laborer than the soldier. With other men from Windham he went to coastal New London and spent his time building a fortification on the summit of Town Hill; this little work mounting six small cannons was supplemental to the larger Fort Trumbull, on the New London side of Connecticut's Thames River. With Fort Griswold on the Groton side, Fort Trumbull guarded the approaches to the towns and protected their wharves and shipping. The fort on Town Hill overlooked Fort Trumbull and could conceivably bombard it if the large work fell to the enemy, but the effectiveness of such an action was questionable and the small fort provided little protection against a landward assault on its larger neighbor. Because of this apparent uselessness the soldiers building it called it Fort Nonesuch, Fort Nonsense, or Fort Folly, and it was never given an official name. Daniel Waldo made only a small contribution to the earth-and-timber fortification which was completed late in 1779. Two years later it was tested when British troops under Benedict Arnold landed on both sides of the river and advanced over land toward the two large forts. An epic battle ensued at Fort Griswold, but on the New London side the attackers bypassed little Fort Nonesuch; it wasn't even manned. The small garrison of Fort Trumbull abandoned the work and fled across the river to join the defenders of the other fort.

Daniel Waldo had no involvement with Fort Nonesuch after May 1779. Released from his one-month obligation, his activities go unrecorded until he joined the militia once again in April 1780. Connecticut's militia was well organized, formed into regiments from various regions of the colony. These regiments were raised and disbanded annually and spent much of the war along the coast keeping a watchful eye on enemy movements in Long Island Sound, ever vigilant for incursions of any sort. In 1780 the men

1. Charles J. Hoadley, trans., *The Public Records of the Colony of Connecticut* (Hartford: Case, Lockwood & Brainard Co., 1887), 3–4.

Photograph of Daniel Waldo by Daniel Dennison, Albany, NY, taken in 1862 to commemorate his 100th birthday and bearing his signature on the back (inset); this is one of several poses taken during this session. (*William L. Clements Library*)

from Windham and neighboring towns were organized into a company commanded by Captain Nathaniel Wells, beginning a service obligation of eight months. Expecting to be home again by the last day of the year, the Windham men began their stint with a two-day jaunt to Mill's Tavern in East Hartford. After staying there one night, they headed toward Horse Neck in the area of Greenwich, Connecticut, passing through Hartford, Wallingford, North Haven, and New Haven. At Fairfield they spent a few days training, something sorely needed before going on through Norwalk to the coastal post at Horse Neck.[2]

In Horse Neck they joined with other militia companies and formed a regiment commanded by Lt. Col. Levi Wells. It was hardly a cohesive fighting force. Many of the new enlistees had seen several years of service in the war, some fighting in important campaigns and seeing famous battles like the defeat of General Burgoyne's army in 1777 and the struggle at Monmouth, New Jersey, in 1778. But many others were men like Daniel Waldo with little experience or none at all, unaccustomed not only to battle but to the military routine of hygiene, discipline, vigilance, and long marches. Each man probably had a measure of skill in handling a firearm, but not in the coordinated, mutually supporting activities that are essential to successful military operations. And within two weeks of their initial formation, the regiment was stationed at an active, dangerous frontline post on the Connecticut shoreline. The 46-year-old Lt. Col. Wells was a seasoned officer, having served in the French and Indian War and in the current war since 1775 (including several months as a prisoner of war after the battle of Long Island in 1776), but his task of maintaining a capable regiment in a dangerous location was daunting.

The post at Horse Neck near the town of Greenwich marked the western edge of American-held territory along the coast. A dozen miles to the west were British forces in New Rochelle. The entire region between New York City and Connecticut had never been fully in the hands of either side from the time the British garrisoned New York in 1776. The Continental army maintained a substantial encampment in the region of Redding while the British

2. Pension deposition of Nehamiah Ripley, W. 1489, Revolutionary War Pensions.

held Manhattan and Long Island; each side pushed toward the other's lines with some frequency. The post at Horse Neck was important for maintaining observation over British movements through the waters of Long Island Sound, for any maritime advance on the Connecticut coast would have to pass by this post; it also guarded the most direct overland approach to the encampments in Redding. The post had gained importance early in 1779 when a British force marched into the place, destroying military positions at Horse Neck and the salt works in Greenwich; American General Israel Putnam, who had been visiting the outposts, made a narrow escape that is still commemorated in the region. A few months later British forces raided Norwalk, Fairfield, and New Haven. When the militia under Wells arrived at Horse Neck at the beginning of the 1780 campaign season, they knew that they were the first line of defense against similar incursions expected that year.

For their first several weeks in Horse Neck the militiamen changed quarters frequently, sometimes sheltering in houses and sometimes camping at different locations in the woods. This irregular lodging was a defensive measure to prevent any patterns of behavior that could lead to a nighttime attack by the enemy. By the middle of the summer, however, another regiment arrived and the whole force, now numbering some 600 men, established a regular encampment. Lt. Col. Wells sent patrols west to probe British positions near New Rochelle and diligently sent intelligence reports to the senior officer in overall command of the posts north and east of New York, Major General Benedict Arnold.[3] There is no evidence telling which specific soldiers participated in these missions, so we can't say whether Waldo was actively involved.

In late July British regiments began moving and fears rose that some sort of attack was imminent. On August 1 the regiments at Horse Neck were ordered to join a larger force in the vicinity of White Plains and they promptly were on the move; the next day they received orders to divest themselves of all heavy baggage so that they could move as rapidly as possible, but to remain where

3. Correspondence between Levi Wells and Benedict Arnold, August and September 1780, George Washington Papers, Library of Congress, memory.loc.gov/ammem/gwhtml/gwhome.html.

they were and await further instructions. They encamped about five miles north of their previous post and remained for a week or two before returning to Horse Neck. At the beginning of September they marched out again, this time to North Castle, northeast of White Plains, again in coordination with other parts of the army; once again they soon returned to their encampment near Greenwich.

The haste and severity of these marches is characterized by one instance where the militia regiment marched out and back over the course of two days with no provisions at all. It had begun raining in the morning, and they arrived at their encampment late in the afternoon where they prepared a hasty meal consisting only of boiled beef, but were also given an extra allowance of rum. At 9 P.M. they received orders to march yet again toward New Rochelle, and they set off in the rainy darkness. Not enough food and too much rum soon took their toll; after a few miles the weary, tipsy soldiers could march no more, and they found whatever comfort they could in the rainy woods. A well-timed attack would have meant disaster, but there was no way for the enemy to know the sorry state of the militiamen hunkered down in the rain; by morning they had sobered sufficiently to return to the encampment at Horse Neck.

Another alarm came in late September when they received sudden orders to march toward West Point. General Arnold had been discovered in the traitorous act of attempting to hand over the important post to the enemy, and fear of a sudden British advance up the Hudson River ran high. By the time they had gone only half way, however, things had settled down sufficiently and they dutifully returned to their encampment once more. Although Arnold's treason threw the region's military situation into temporary disarray, it came near the end of the campaign season, and once it became clear that British designs on West Point were foiled, the entire area gradually calmed down.

By December, the soldiers in Lt. Col. Wells's regiment were breathing easier. They'd made it through the campaign season with much tension but few actual brushes with the enemy. The imminent threats had passed. Armies on both sides prepared for winter. The weather turned sharply colder and the end of the Connecticut soldiers' enlistments drew near. Daniel Waldo and his

comrades moved from tents into quarters, lodging in neighborhood houses and inns. They no doubt looked forward to being discharged at the end of the month, their eight-month obligations
over, the Connecticut shoreline secure until the next campaign season; they could relax for a few weeks and go home at the end of
the year.

That's when the attack came.

On the night of December 9–10 a corps of loyalist cavalrymen
known as the Westchester Refugees under the command of
Colonel James DeLancey took the billeted soldiers completely by
surprise.[4] They had advanced rapidly from British lines, twenty-
five horses each carrying one dragoon and one infantryman. Well
informed of the American positions, they divided into groups and
assaulted each of three buildings housing Wells's men at about 3
A.M. It all happened quickly. Men who resisted were cut down, not
by gunfire but by sabers, felled by multiple cuts on the head, arms,
and upper body and then trampled by horses. Sentries had no
chance to sound an alarm. Soldiers who turned out of a barn where
they'd been asleep were immediately surrounded by horsemen.
Daniel Waldo stood sentry at the door of the house where Lt. Col.
Wells and several other officers were quartered; he heard no warnings from out-sentries and was surprised by an enemy soldier who
attempted to shoot him, only to have the musket misfire. Waldo
laid down his weapon but still his assailant thrust at him with a
bayonet. Waldo then laid down himself, and the loyalists stormed
the house. Waldo, along with everyone inside, was taken prisoner.
Having made a prize of six officers including Lt. Col. Wells, the
Refugees quickly retreated the thirty miles back to their own lines,
having suffered not a single casualty.

In his own pension deposition, Daniel Waldo says little about
this wild melee except that he was a sentry at one of the doors and
was taken prisoner. Perhaps he understated the event because, as
he told the man who photographed him years later, he himself put

4. Information about the raid is drawn from the pension depositions of John
Haskell, S. 21809 (including the deposition of William Bainard); Caleb Thomas,
W. 6273; and newspaper accounts in the *Connecticut Journal*, December 14, 1780;
Royal Gazette (New York), December 16, 1780; and *New Jersey Gazette*, December
20, 1780.

up no resistance. If he felt any embarrassment about this he need not have; it's clear that the whole affair happened quickly, and those who did try to fight suffered terribly for their temerity. One of Waldo's fellow soldiers was "wounded by a Cutlass in the head, & trodden upon by their horses,"[5] while another received "three wounds by cutlasses on the head one wound on his shoulder, whereby the shoulder blade was laid bare also one wound on the upper side of the arm and one on the lower arm bone, it being laid bare, also one in the knee by which the knee pan was separated from the adjacent parts," crippling him for life.[6] These awful wounds were typical of the nighttime raids conducted by both armies on the shores of Long Island Sound, reflecting not savagery on the part of one side or the other but the harsh reality of rapid incursions conducted in darkness.

A mere twenty-one days before the end of his eight-month enlistment, Daniel Waldo was taken to New York and incarcerated in the infamous Sugar House prison. Originally built as a sugar refinery, this large stone structure had been used to hold prisoners of war since the British occupied the city in late 1776. Crowded conditions were a constant problem largely because the British usually had many prisoners and few places to put them; they also held in low esteem the captives who were rebels against the British government rather than soldiers of a recognized foreign nation. The dank, dark, overcrowded facility bred disease that spread easily among undernourished prisoners.[7] Waldo gave no description of his time there in his pension deposition, and apparently the only information related to Rev. Hillard about his incarceration was that provisions were scant; he made no other recorded mention of what he experienced there. Whatever his lot, it was better than that of naval prisoners held on the infamous prison ships in New York harbor where conditions were far worse.

5. Pension deposition of Ebenezer Chapman, W. 17618, Revolutionary War Pensions.

6. Pension deposition of Lemuel King, W. 26179, Revolutionary War Pensions.

7. A detailed account of life in the Sugar House, albeit a few years earlier than Waldo was there, can be found in Charles Bushnell, *Narrative of the Life and Adventures of Levi Hanford, a Soldier of the Revolution* (New York: Privately printed, 1863), 13–23.

If Waldo was unlucky to have been captured so close to the end of his enlistment, he was lucky to have been made a prisoner at that time of the war. After only two months, an exchange was agreed upon; the British released a number of prisoners for a like number released by their adversaries. Exchanges such as these occurred frequently during the war, although many captured soldiers spent far more time as prisoners than Waldo did. He and his comrades captured at Horse Neck were released from the Sugar House and conveyed to Staten Island, then to Elizabeth Town in New Jersey[8]–not a convenient location for these Connecticut men, but it nonetheless took them only a few days of overland travel to get around north of New York City, across the Hudson River, and back to their hometowns.[9] They had missed the disbanding of their regiment and because of this received no written discharge papers, but they were able to collect the pay that was due to them.[10]

This was the end of Daniel Waldo's military career. Although the war continued, he never again enlisted nor was drafted for further militia service. The record given in his pension deposition misstates the year of his second term of service as 1779 rather than 1780; the date of the Horse Neck raid at which he was captured, known with certainty from a variety of sources, provides the key from which the remaining dates can be determined accurately, and other pension depositions confirm that the year was 1780. It may be that Waldo himself, five decades after the fact, confused the year of his capture with the more famous Horse Neck raid in 1779 that was well known for General Putnam's storied escape. Waldo also is incorrect by two weeks about the day on which he was captured. Rev. Hillard compounds the temporal errors, putting his initial militia service in 1778; this is probably a mistaken attempt to reconcile Waldo's misstatement that both his first and second terms

8. Pension deposition of Caleb Thomas, W. 6273, Revolutionary War Pensions.

9. This seems to have been a typical manner for the British to release prisoners, sending New England men to New Jersey and men from other colonies to Connecticut; see Charles Bushnell, *Narrative of the Life and Adventures of Levi Hanford*, 31.

10. Pension deposition of Ebenezer Chapman, W. 17618, Revolutionary War Pensions.

Livingston's Sugar House on Crown Street (today's Liberty Street) in New York City, used as a prison during the American Revolution. (*Museum of the City of New York*)

of service began in 1779. Regardless, the shifting of events by one year is the only significant error in both Waldo's own deposition and Hillard's telling of Waldo's military career. Although generally accurate, both accounts suffer from understating the daily hardships that Waldo experienced.

Hillard's account of Daniel Waldo's postmilitary life is succinct and accurate. In addition to what Hillard tells us, we know that Waldo applied for a pension by giving his deposition to a probate court in Lebanon, Connecticut, on July 28, 1832. One fellow applicant testified to having served with him in New London in 1779. Other documents filed with his pension deposition give a few additional anecdotes. After Waldo moved to New York in 1837, he applied for a new pension certificate because his original document "on or about the 25th Day of April 1837 he lost somewhere between Hartford Connecticut and Newark New York having his papers in his surtout pocket when he left Hartford he concludes they worked out of his pocket into the stage or were stolen by some passenger he therefore prays that a new certificate may be issued to him."[11] The file includes some letters from the same era dealing with the transfer of his pension from Connecticut to New York, and later documents transferring it to Washington, D.C., for a time and then back to New York.

In January 1852, a New York City resident put a notice in the newspaper that he was in possession of a cane made of wood from a beam of the long-demolished Sugar House prison. He wanted to give the artifact to a living survivor of incarceration in that place; he invited any such men to contact him, and would draw lots to determine the recipient if more than one applied. He received five applications, suggesting that only five former prisoners remained alive that year. We can only speculate as to whether Daniel Waldo was among the applicants, for he was not the winner and the other four names were not recorded.[12]

It bears noting that although Hillard visited Waldo, he was unable to interview the aged veteran due to a sudden decline in health after a fall; fortunately Nelson Moore had captured Waldo's image before this sad event, and related to Hillard some of what Waldo had told him. Only weeks after Rev. Hillard visited him, Daniel Waldo died on July 20, 1864.

---

11. A surtout was a type of overcoat; by "stage" Waldo refers to a stage coach.
12. Charles Bushnell, *Narrative of the Life and Adventures of Levi Hanford*, 42.

It is unlikely that Daniel Waldo wore any type of uniform during either of his two stints as a soldier in the Connecticut militia. He served for one month in 1779 when he was sixteen years old, and again for most of the following year on the Connecticut coast at Horse Neck. These men who turned out for a few months at a time probably wore the most serviceable garments they could bring with them from home. Being mostly from rural farming communities, they were certainly accustomed to local travel and working outdoors in harsh conditions, and probably had clothing well suited for many days of hard labor at a stretch; how well it held up to months of continuous military service, however, is open to question. Neither Waldo nor any of his fellow soldiers made much mention of clothing and equipment in their pension depositions, even when describing hardships that they'd encountered. Perhaps they were always sufficiently clothed, with repairs or replacement garments available from local sources or delivered from home.

The soldier depicted here wears a long single-breasted coat, probably of inexpensive brown, dark blue or grey woolen broadcloth, designed to button snugly for warmth when necessary. He wears a woolen waistcoat over his linen shirt, and knee-length woolen breeches with long stockings, all common for both civilian and military wear. He has no gaiters or leggings to keep mud and debris out of his shoes, indicating that he is not prepared for a march. The only thing that distinguishes him as a soldier is the cartridge pouch slung over his left shoulder that holds easily-accessible ammunition. His musket is American made but patterned after British military muskets. Young Daniel Waldo's only exposure to combat, while he was posted sentry at the door of his officers' quarters, left him in a compromising position.

For more on civilian clothing of the era, see Linda Baumgarten, *What Clothes Reveal: the Language of Clothing in Colonial and Federal America* (New Haven: Yale University Press, 2002).

Drawing by Eric H. Schnitzer

The Pension Deposition of Daniel Waldo[13]

APPEARED IN PROBATE COURT ON 28 JULY 1832, LEBANON, CT

Daniel Waldo a Clergyman resident in Lebanon aforesaid in the County of New London and State of Connecticut aged sixty-nine years on the 10 day of September last who being first duly sworn according to Law doth on his Oath make the following declaration in order to obtain the benefit of the Act of Congress passed June 7 1832.

That he entered the service of the United State under the following named Officers and served as herein stated. In the month of April 1779 I was drafted into a Company of Connecticut militia under the command of Captain William Howard of Hampton in the County of Windham and performed a tour of duty of one month at New London the company was not annexed to any regiment whilst out but was occupied near New London in building a Fort (back of the town) which was named by the soldiers (by way of ridicule) Fort Nonesuch. My Lieutenant and Ensign I do not recollect. I resided at the time of being drafted as afore said in Windham Windham County and stated aforesaid. At the expiration of the month for which I was drafted I returned to reside Windham [sic]. In the month of April 1779 a company of Connecticut state troops was formed in said Windham under the command of Captain Nathaniel Wales of said Windham into which company I enlisted. In the month of June following said company was annexed to a regiment under the command of Colonel Levi Wells. We were marched to a place then called Horseneck near Greenwich in Connecticut. We were employed in scouting parties and in guarding the country whilst on the 25 day of December 1779 I was stationed as a centinel at the door of the house of Colonel Wells. I together with twenty or more including the said Colonel were taken prisoners by the refugees or cow boys. We were kept prisoners two months to wit until the 25 day of February 1780 in the Sugar house in New York. We were taken prisoner some time in the latter part of December 1780 and were

13. Pension deposition of Daniel Waldo, S. 14782, Revolutionary War Pensions.

exchanged in the latter part of February following. I was born in Windham aforesaid in the year 1762 my birth was recorded in my fathers family bible and I believe in the town records of said Windham. I lived at the time of being called into the aforesaid service of said Windham. Since the Revolutionary War I have resided in the principal part of the times in Suffield in Connecticut but being a Preacher of the Gospel I have for short periods of time resided in other places and for about ten years last past I have resided in said Lebanon. I was never a substitute but went in my own name. I received no written discharge and have no documentary evidences. Seabury Manning of said Windham knows of my first tour of duty and Nehemiah Riply also of said Windham was knowing to my second tour of duty whose depositions I have obtained and I know of but one other person living who was knowing to my services whose testimony I can not conveniently obtain. I am acquainted with the Rev. Edward Bull and Doctor Joseph Comstock both of this town who can testify as to my veracity and their belief of my services as aforesaid.

I also depose and say that from length of time by reason of old age and the consequent loss of memory I cannot swear positively as to the precise length of my service but according to the best of my recollection I served not less than the period mentioned below and in the following grades. For eight months I served as a private and for such service I claim a pension.[14]

I hereby relinquish every claim whatever to a pension or annuity except the present and declare that my name is not on the pension roll of the agency of any state. Sworn to and subscribed the day and year aforesaid.

[signed] Daniel Waldo.

---

14. Waldo gave another deposition on April 8, 1833 that read almost identically to the July 28, 1832, deposition, except for the addition of this paragraph.

RESIDENCE of DANIEL WALDO.

LITH. OF BINGHAM & DODD, HARTFORD, CT.

Lithograph of Daniel Waldo's home, Summer 1864, from *Last Men of the Revolution*. (*Society of the Cincinnati*)

Daniel Waldo

From E. B. Hillard, *The Last Men of the Revolution* (1864)

F ROM LUZERNE I PROCEEDED TO SYRACUSE, THE HOME OF THE Rev. Daniel Waldo, the most widely known of the surviving soldiers of the Revolution.

There were many circumstances which rendered the anticipation of a visit to him one of great pleasure and satisfaction. Known, as he was, to all his countrymen, all felt acquainted with him and interested in him; while his intelligence, his wide familiarity with men and events, and, until of late, the full possession and vigor of his faculties, with his eminently social disposition, the freshness of his feelings, and his undiminished interest both in the past and the present, combined to render an interview with him, in prospect, one of the rare privileges of a lifetime. Most painful, therefore, was my disappointment on reaching his house to find the realization of these anticipations forever forbidden; the communion of life, so pleasant and prolonged, forever terminated; its story, told so often and so willingly, to be told no more. The hour so long awaited at last had come. Death was dealing with the old man. Already he had done with earthly things; and, passed into the border realm between the seen world and the unseen, he was awaiting in passive unconsciousness the opening of those mansions in his Father's house, where so long there had been prepared for him a home.

A fall down a flight of steps, a short time before, though resulting in no immediate bodily injury, gave such a shock to his nervous system that he sunk under it; and his life, already enfeebled by his extreme age, ebbed quietly and painlessly away. The sight of him, as he lay upon his dying bed, was beautiful and touching. It was like the slumber of a child. His look was as peaceful and pleasant as when in health; and upon his wasting features there rested the serene and sweet expression of gentle goodness, breaking, for the moment, into a smile, as, on being addressed, he roused to answer, and then sank again into his dreamless sleep; and as you gazed you no longer wondered at the tender and devoted affection which you saw manifested towards him in that home. To see him, even without knowing him, was to love him; and as he lay there, so loved and tended not only with earthly ministries, but, as you could not doubt, with heavenly, the promise, so precious to the believer, seemed already, by anticipation, fulfilled. Already he had entered into rest. A short time after, on Saturday, the 30th of July, at half-past one in the afternoon, he breathed his last. His age was one hundred and one years, ten months, and twenty days.

Daniel Waldo was born in Windham, (Scotland Parish,) Conn., on the 10th of September, 1762. He was the son of Zaccheus and Tabitha (Kingsbury) Waldo, and was the ninth of thirteen children. His native town will be remembered as the scene of the famous "Battle of the Frogs" and the fright of the inhabitants thereupon, which formed so favorite a theme of the humorous ballad literature of the pre-revolutionary period.[15] The old meeting-house, too, is well known, through the curious and amusing description of it given by President Dwight in his "Travels." "The spot," he writes, "where it is posited bears not a little resemblance to a pound, and it appears as if those who pitched upon it intended to shut the church out of the town and the inhabitants out of the church."[16]

The earliest ancestor of Mr. Waldo in this country was Deacon Cornelius Waldo, of Ipswich, as early as 1654. The line of descent is as follows: Deacon Cornelius; John, of Boston, the first Windham settler; Deacon Edward; Zaccheus; and Rev. Daniel. In the female line he was connected, through his great-grandmother, Rebecca Adams, with the family to which Presidents John and

15. According to legend, during the French and Indian War when many of Windham's able-bodied men were away in the army, the townspeople were aroused one night by frightful wailing sounds from the nearby woods. Fearful of an Indian attack, they fired their weapons blindly into the woods. The next morning they discovered that the sounds were from bullfrogs. William Weaver, *The Battle of the Frogs, at Windham, 1758: With Various Accounts and Three of the Most Popular Ballads on the Subject* (Willimantic, CT: James Walden, 1857).

16. Pound, a high-walled stone enclosure used to hold stray livestock until an owner claimed it. This passage is from Timothy Dwight, *Travels in New England and New York,* 4 vols. (1821–1822); Dwight was a president of Yale University.

John Quincy Adams belonged.[17] At the time of his death, he was the oldest native of Windham; and at the last commencement of Yale College, he was reported as the oldest living graduate, belonging to the class of 1788.

His connection with the war of the Revolution begun in 1778. In that year, being then sixteen years old, he was drafted as a soldier for a month's service at New London. He subsequently enlisted for eight months in the service of the State; and during the term of this enlistment, in March, 1779, was taken prisoner by the tories at Horseneck. This will be recollected as the spot rendered famous by Putnam's escape, on horseback, down the stone steps from the height on which the continental troops were posted.[18] The circumstances of Mr. Waldo's capture, as given by himself to the artist who took his photograph, were as follows: One of the guards, on leaving his beat one stormy night, failed to give him warning, and thus the tories surprised him. One of them snapped a musket at him, but it only flashed in the pan; whereupon he laid down his own musket and made signs of surrender. But one of the enemy, on pretense that he was about to pick it up again, made a thrust at him with his bayonet, which failed to pierce him. He thereupon demanded to be treated as a prisoner of war; and lying down, the attacking party passed over him into the house which he was guarding, capturing the whole company (thirty-seven in number) which it contained. With his fellow prisoners Mr. Waldo was carried to New York, where he was confined in the far-famed "Sugar House" for about two months. There, with the exception of short rations, he was well treated. This terminated his immediate connection with the war. Upon his release by exchange, he returned to his home, in Windham, and resumed his labors on the farm.

17. For more on Waldo's heritage, see Joseph D. Hall, *The Genealogy and Biography of the Waldos of America* (Danielsonville, CT: Scofield and Hamilton, 1883).

18. In February 1779 General Israel Putnam was visiting American posts in Horse Neck when the area suddenly came under attack. The legend is that Putnam made a narrow escape by riding his horse down a steep, rocky slope. Daniel Cruson, *Putnam's Revolutionary War Winter Encampment: The History and Archaeology of Putnam Memorial State Park* (Charleston, SC: History Press, 2011), 80–81.

At the age of about twenty, becoming hopefully a Christian, he resolved to devote himself to the ministry; and after a brief period spent in preparation, he entered Yale College, and graduated, with honors, in 1788. He was a member, while in college, of its most ancient literary society, the Linonian. Among his classmates were Dr. Chapin, of Rocky Hill; James Lanman, U.S. Senator from Connecticut; and the eminent Jeremiah Mason, of Massachusetts, with whom he roomed during the last two years of his college life. He studied theology, after the manner of his time, with Rev. Dr. Hart, of Preston; and, after about a year spent in the study, was licensed to preach by the Windham Association, October 13, 1789. After preaching in several places, for a short time in each, he was ordained on the 24th of May, 1792, as pastor of the church at West Suffield, where he remained eighteen years. Here he was married to Mary Hanchett, by whom he had five children. In 1805, Mrs. Waldo became insane, and died seven years ago, after having been in this state uninterruptedly for upwards of fifty years. "I lived," said the old man, in speaking of it, "fifty years with a crazy wife."

On leaving Suffield, Mr. Waldo went to Columbia, where he preached a few Sabbaths. While there, a military review took place, and Mr. Waldo was invited to dine with the company. At the table there was a good deal of swearing; and upon the captain remarking to Mr. Waldo, in the course of the dinner, that he was glad he had come to dine with them, and that in this he differed from some of his brethren who had declined similar invitations, Mr. Waldo, raising his voice so as to be heard by all present, replied, "My Master was not afraid to dine with publicans and sinners, and I am not." As may be supposed, there was no more swearing during the dinner.

Early in the present century, Mr. Waldo made some missionary tours, in the employ of the Missionary Society of Connecticut, to the states of New York and Pennsylvania,–at that time the "Far West." In 1811, he went, under the patronage of the Society for promoting Christian Knowledge, to Rhode Island, where he labored nine years. Then, for a few months, in 1820, he supplied the pulpit in Harvard, Massachusetts; after which he returned to Connecticut, and in a short time became pastor of the church in Exeter, where he remained twelve years.

In 1835, he removed to the state of New York, where his son had settled a short time before. In 1856, he accompanied his son's family to Syracuse, where he spent the remainder of his days. For more than seventy years he was a minister in the Congregational Church.

On the 22d of December, 1856, upon the motion of Hon. Mr. Granger, the representative from his district, Mr. Waldo being then ninety-six years of age, was chosen chaplain of the House of Representatives; to which honorable position he was re-elected the following year.

During the exercise of this office he was called to preach the funeral sermon of Preston Brooks, the ruffian assailant of Hon. Charles Sumner, which he did from the text, "To-day shalt thou be with me in Paradise."[19] Upon what principle this text was selected is not known. Upon reflection, it occurs that the point of connection may be the circumstance that the words were originally addressed to a malefactor. While connected with Congress, he spent most of his time in reading, which he greatly loved–not wishing, as he used to say, to hear "the quarrels in the House." On the Sabbath after he had completed his century he preached in the Second Presbyterian church, Albany, a sermon which he had just prepared, and which, it is said, would have done no discredit to him in the meridian of his life.[20] His last sermon was preached after he had entered upon his one hundred and second year.

Mr. Waldo never saw either Washington or La Fayette. He served for a short time as chaplain at New London, in the year 1812. In the present conflict with rebellion he was intensely loyal, greatly desiring to live till the rebellion should be suppressed. He had implicit faith in the ultimate success of the Union arms and the re-establishment of the authority of the National Government over all the states. President Lincoln he deemed honest, but not decided enough. He thought that the leaders of the rebellion should be dealt with in such a manner that no one would dare, in the future, to repeat the experiment.

In his personal habits Mr. Waldo was very careful and regular. His standing advice was to "eat little." He drank tea and coffee. The

19. On May 22, 1856, Representative Preston Smith Brooks of South Carolina assaulted Senator Charles Sumner of Massachusetts on the Senate floor. For more on this see Stephen Puleo, *The Caning: The Assault That Drove America to Civil War* (Yardley, PA: Westholme Publishing, 2012).

20. In other words, the sermon Waldo gave when he was 100 years old would have done him credit even at 50.

control of the temper he deemed one of the most important conditions of health, declaring that a fit of passion does more to break down the constitution than a fever. His mental vigor he retained wonderfully to the last. His memory was excellent, differing from that of most aged people, in that he retained current events with the same clearness as the earlier incidents of his history.

The closing years of Mr. Waldo's life were passed in great comfort, in the family of his son. Everything that affection could prompt or refinement suggest, he there enjoyed. His pension, until the last year of his life, had been ninety-six dollars a year; a hundred dollars was added to it a few months before he died. But this was not needed to secure to him every condition possible of the enjoyment of life. The tenderest ministries of filial affection were bestowed upon him. Of these, a lock of his hair lying before me, soft, silvery, silky, is mute but touching witness. The circle of his friends embraced not only the best society of the city where he dwelt, but the eminent and noble of the land. Wherever he appeared in public, it was only to receive the sincerest honors which a grateful and loving people could pay him; and in his death he is regretted by all. He lived long to witness and enjoy the greatness and glory of his country; and his death was graciously delayed till its still loftier greatness and higher glory were assured.

The words of one who knew him intimately, and who has recorded his life more worthily, will fitly close this sketch:

> Mr. Waldo possessed naturally a clear, sound, well balanced mind, with little of the metaphysical or the imaginative. He was a great reader, eagerly devouring every work of interest that came within his reach. His spirit was eminently kind and genial, and this, united with his keen wit and large stores of general knowledge, made him a most agreeable companion. He was one of the most contented of mortals. Though he experienced many severe afflictions, and had always from an early period of his ministry one of the heaviest burdens of domestic sorrow resting upon him, his calm confidence in God never forsook him, nor was he ever heard to utter a murmuring word. As a preacher, he was luminous, direct, and eminently practical; his manner was simple and earnest, and well fitted to command attention. At the close of a life of more than a hundred years, there is no passage in his history which those who loved him would wish to have erased.

DANIEL WALDO.

Daniel Waldo, photographed by Messrs. N. A. and R. A. Moore, 1864. (*Society of the Cincinnati*)

Lemuel Cook

2nd Dragoons

A WEEK AFTER CONNECTICUT MILITIAMAN DANIEL WALDO WAS taken prisoner at Horse Neck, another Connecticut teenager took up arms and joined a fight that must have seemed to be focusing more and more on his home colony. Lemuel Cook was a farm boy from the town of Northbury, an inland community in the western part of the state. Although not near any front line, the region had seen its share of excitement. In 1777 a British raid had destroyed military stores in nearby Danbury; 1779 had seen incursions on New Haven, Fairfield, and Norwalk, coastal towns just a day or two's journey away. Smaller actions like the one in which Waldo was taken were common. Major American posts along the Hudson River were not far to the west, and Northbury was on the route from there to Hartford, Providence, and Boston. There were probably traces of the war in the form of passing soldiers, supplies, and prisoners almost every day. Certainly the conflict, which had been going on for nearly six years by December 1780, was a constant topic of news, rumor, and conversation.

Not long after his sixteenth birthday,[1] Lemuel Cook chose to enlist not in the militia but the full-time army; he joined the 2nd Dragoons, a corps of cavalry commanded by Colonel Elisha Sheldon.[2] The army had only a few cavalry units; the nature of this American war made it unnecessary to have large numbers of mounted troops, but a skilled cadre was essential. One trooper in

1. Lemuel Cook's birth date is not known. When he deposed for a pension in 1818 he gave his age as 52, and in 1820 gave it as 55. Obituary notices in 1866 generally gave his age as 102, but some said 104 and at least one source reported 107. Given that he enlisted as soon as he was old enough, 16 years of age, and his enlistment is known to have been in December 1780, we can be confident that he was born in 1764.

2. Modern sources often call the regiment the 2nd Continental Light Dragoons, but this terminology does not appear in documents contemporary to the organization's existence; in primary sources it is generally called the 2nd Dragoons, 2nd Light Dragoons, Sheldon's Light Horse, or other variations.

the regiment wrote that "the duties performed by the light horse were performed in various places–and were various–patrolling, mounting guard, employed as expresses."[3] Although few in number, they figured in almost every camp and campaign, particularly in their role of gathering information (by being able to get into and out of hostile territory quickly) and transmitting it (by rapidly carrying messages from one command to another).

The Dragoons were well equipped and made a fine appearance. Troopers on horseback, dressed in blue coats trimmed in white, helmets with white horsehair crests, armed with swords and pistols, they were surely an alluring sight to a teenager with martial aspirations. They were experienced, too. The regiment was authorized in December 1776, among the first corps authorized by Congress as a Continental regiment; as such, it had not been disbanded and raised anew several times like most infantry regiments. In the ranks were men who had seen the disastrous defeats at Long Island and White Plains in 1776 (while serving in other regiments before the 2nd Dragoons was raised), and had participated in victories at Saratoga in 1777 and Monmouth in 1778. The regiment's major, Benjamin Tallmadge, was active in General Washington's intelligence-gathering network, maintaining contacts deep inside British-held territory. Parties of the 2nd Dragoons used whaleboats to conduct patrols and raids on the Long Island shore across from Connecticut.[4] Detachments of the regiment were frequently in close proximity to General Washington and other senior officers, providing both protection and rapid conveyance of information. A French aide-de-camp, accustomed to seeing professional European soldiers, called the 2nd Dragoons "incontestably the best troops on the continent."[5]

Lemuel Cook, with no previous military experience but undoubtedly with great youthful zeal, joined the regiment while it was in winter quarters in Simsbury and Windsor, Connecticut.

---

3. Pension deposition of Luke Guyant, S. 17990, Revolutionary War Pensions.

4. Much of the regiment's activities are discussed in Benjamin Tallmadge, *Memoir* (New York: Thomas Holman, 1858).

5. Journal of Jean-François-Louis, Comte de Clermont-Crèvecœur, in Howard C. Rice and Anne S. K. Brown, trans., *The American Campaigns of Rochambeau's Army* (Providence, RI: Brown University Press, 1972), 1:31.

Many new troopers enlisted during these winter months, and training was probably intensive. A substantial force of French troops had landed in Rhode Island in the summer of 1780 and spent the winter there. No one doubted that this reinforcement to the Continental Army would bring major developments in 1781, but the dragoons in Connecticut could assume only that they'd have an active campaign season without knowing any specifics of what awaited them.

Cook was enlisted by Captain George Hurlbut. Young and not fully grown, he was told by the captain that he must enlist for the duration of the war rather than for the three-year term offered to some men. This was apparently the officer's way of justifying acceptance of an undersized recruit; at five feet five inches tall, Cook was among the shortest men in regiment when he enlisted. Studying the surviving documents concerning the 2nd Dragoons, it is challenging to reconcile the details of Cook's military career. The regiment consisted of six troops, four of which were mounted cavalry troopers and two of which were foot soldiers called light infantry. Cook related to Rev. Hillard that he served in one of the light infantry troops commanded by Captain William Staunton, and he does in fact appear in an undated regimental book among the soldiers of the 6th Troop commanded by that officer. But just days after Cook enlisted, the regiment was reorganized and Staunton took command of one of the mounted troops.[6] Further, Cook mentions having brought his own horse from home and spoke of General Washington's admiration of his "smart mount." Regimental orders suggest that men were moved from the dismounted to the mounted troops when horses became available for them; examination of all of the pension depositions of men who served in the regiment, compared to the available regimental books and muster rolls, reveals that men were in fact transferred from one troop to another albeit for unstated reasons. Unless Cook simply remembered incorrectly, we must assume that he had no horse when he enlisted but had gotten one from his family farm by the summer of 1781, a plausible notion because the regiment was never far from his home during those months.

6. Regimental orders for December 20, 1780. Orderly book, 2nd Dragoons, Mss A 1103, New England Historical and Genealogical Society.

It didn't take long for Cook and the other young dragoons to become involved in the war. The regiment moved to the Continental Army cantonment on the west side of the Hudson River at New Windsor, New York in April 1781; by July they were part of the extensive summer encampment established on the east side of the river extending inland from Dobbs Ferry. This ground was chosen as the place where the Continental Army under Washington would meet their new French allies under Comte de Rochambeau which were marching west from Rhode Island. The combined force would, it was hoped, be capable of mounting a credible assault on the British garrison entrenched in and around New York City, finally breaking the stalemate that had persisted for years. Enthusiasm was high.

As the lead elements of the French army arrived in late June, Washington devised a reconnaissance in force to threaten the strategic British post at Kingsbridge on the north end of Manhattan Island, and to head off a suspected British attack on his own positions. The 2nd Dragoons were deployed on the American left, the easternmost side of the lines, along with their French equivalents, Lauzun's Legion. Initially their task was to suppress any opposition east of the Harlem River while a substantial force of infantry moved against King's Bridge in the dark on the moonless night of July 2–3. The fortunes of war, however, intervened; a force of German troops was already operating that night around White Plains between the British and American lines. The unsuspecting forces met each other and a series of sharp actions ensued; American infantry pushed the Germans back across the bridge to Manhattan, but daylight brought a German counterattack with cavalry and infantry that drove the Americans up Valentine's Hill, almost two miles north of the bridge and site of the battle of White Plains in 1776. The exact tide of the battle is difficult to ascertain from accounts of individuals who participated, but the upshot was that the cavalry on the American left raced to Valentine's Hill to support the infantry now defending it from the German attack, and American infantry poured in from the north to further reinforce the position. Faced with overwhelming opposition, the Germans retired back to King's Bridge by the end of the day on July 3. With all forces back at more or less their original positions, the battle had no real consequence and has been all but forgotten even though it was a moderate-sized action compared to others in the war. Although some of his comrades referred to it only as a skirmish, and indeed the cavalry's role seems to have been small and occurred late in the action, it was Lemuel Cook's first exposure to battle, an experience he remembered for the rest of his life.

During the next couple of days, Washington and Rochambeau reconnoitered the British lines, escorted by American and French dragoons. At one point they got caught by rising waters on a small coastal island; Rochambeau himself recounted the technique that his professional French cavalry learned from their new American allies:

> In this reconnoitering we tried the American plan of making the horses swim across a river, by collecting them in a drove after the manner of wild horses. . . . Two small boats were brought to us, in which we embarked with the saddles and harness of the horses; then two American dragoons were sent ahead, who led by the bridles two horses that were good swimmers; these were followed by all the rest, who were urged on by the cracking of the whips of some dragoons who remained on the other side, and to whom we sent back the boats.[7]

With the French army encamped alongside the Americans on the east side of the Hudson and planning under way for an assault on New York, General Washington maintained a broader view of changing developments across all theaters of the war. Although taking New York would be the grandest possible achievement, it became clear that the necessary land and naval forces could not be assembled in a timely manner. On the other hand, a strong French fleet was moving to the Chesapeake Bay, and British forces in the south were concentrating at a small Virginia post called Yorktown. In mid-August, Washington took a great strategic gamble and redirected his efforts to the south. With remarkable speed, he orchestrated a brilliant shift of operations, moving a substantial portion of his army through New Jersey under the guise of threatening New York from the south by way of Staten Island. At the same time, he directed the French fleet to send transport ships up the

7. *Memoirs of the Marshall Count de Rochambeau,* M. W. E. Wright, trans. (Paris: French, English and American Library, 1838), 58–59.

Chesapeake Bay so his troops could quickly leave New Jersey, board the vessels at Head of Elk in Maryland, and set upon the British army in Virginia. This massive military operation was planned and effected in only a matter of weeks; by mid-September American and French forces were preparing to besiege Yorktown, with the French fleet blocking any British retreat by sea. It was a masterstroke that veterans of the war continued to talk about throughout their lives.[8]

The 2nd Dragoons as a regiment remained behind when Washington moved southward, but a small detachment, about eighteen troopers, accompanied the campaign army. The need for such a detachment was clear: dragoons were always in demand so that senior officers could send and receive messages quickly, and an army on the move was liable to need them more than ever. Not clear, however, is why the young, relatively inexperienced Lemuel Cook was among this select detachment. The five others who have been identified all had been in the regiment almost since it was formed and by August 1781 had four or more years of military experience, compared to Cook's eight months.[9] Perhaps there were other new troopers in the detachment; a complete list of them has not been found. Cook's recollections of vignettes on the march south and at Yorktown sound genuine, though, and leave us with no doubt that he was actually there and not conflating, in the way that other aged veterans did, his own recollections with the popular memory of famous events.

Service with the dragoons meant exposure to and interaction with the most senior officers of the Continental Army. In later years, as the reputation of George Washington grew to mythic proportions, Lemuel Cook's children, grandchildren, and great-grandchildren repeatedly asked him to relate his encounters with the legendary general. One of the latter recorded a typical response:

8. Michael Cecere, "Washington's Deviation to Virginia," *Journal of the American Revolution*, September 23, 2013, allthingsliberty.com/2013/09/washingtons-deviation-virginia/.

9. Besides Cook, five pensioners mentioned in their depositions having been part of the detachment of the 2nd Dragoons that went to Yorktown. Pension depositions of Luke Guyant, S. 17990; Walter Tiffany, W. 19205; Ethel Plant, S. 43870; Solomon Parkhurst, S. 34463; Samuel Adams, S. 38483; Revolutionary War Pensions.

Where Lemuel Cook lived and died. He was the last survivor of the Revolutionary War. Died May 20, 1866, aged 102 years.

AT CLARENDON. N.Y.

Postcard showing Lemuel Cook's home and an inset image of him. The photographer and date of the inset photograph are not known, but it is not one of those produced by the Moore brothers in 1864. (*Barr Cook*)

I saw General Washington a few times, said a few words to him and he back to me. I'll not forget. First time I set eyes on him was at White Plains or thereabouts. I'd joined up at the first call and those first couple of years were hard ones. Our company was resting near White Plains after being pushed off the Island and out of New York City and up River. My job was with Major Tallmadge, being in the Light Dragoons we had horses to take care of. Mine was a good ole Bay I'd brought from home. I was caring for my horse and a couple of others that needed rubbing down and heard a commotion a ways down the road. I could see by the uniforms it was officers leading several companies of Foot.[10] One fellow sat in the saddle head and shoulders above the others. I knew he must be the General, we had heard how large a man he was. As they came closer all I could do was stand there with my mouth open. An officer in front gave me a dirty look like to be saying, "How Come you don't salute?" I whipped off a good fancy one. The officers dismounted and went to talk with the Major I suppose. I went back to my horse, a while later the General came around the headquarters where I was, to stretch his legs I suppose and said, "Is that your horse soldier?" "Yes, Sir," said I coming to attention. He put me at ease and asked my name, "Lemuel Cook, from Connecticut, Sir." "That's a right smart mount you have there Lemuel Cook from Connecticut." "He's done good by me, General" said I. "Well, you take care of him, you will be glad you did," with that the General went about his business. That's all there was to it, I'll never forget though, all the things that must have been pressing on him he took time for a kind word. He had the kindest look in the eyes I've ever seen. Got the chance to see him a few times more being in the quartermasters, they called us artificers in them days. Didn't see him again until some two, maybe three years later. We were going down thru the Head of Elk, things were better, we had been winning we knew we had a big battle coming up somewhere to the south. Scuttle butt was that the General had gone on ahead and would meet us along the way. We had stopped and I was minding my own business paying no mind to no one when I heard a rich full voice say, "Lem Cook, is that you? I thought that might be you with that Bay." I had whirled around with my eyes bugging out and mouth wide open again, amazed that he

10. Foot, that is, infantry.

had remembered me. I finally managed a "Yes Sir, it's very good to see you Sir." "I admire the lines of your Bay, Lem, I have one like it at Mount Vernon." "Yes Sir, he's a little worse for wear but I've been keeping your advice, my brothers made me promise to bring him back to the farm when there was done." "That's what we are about, Private," and with that the General was gone as quickly as he appeared. I'd grown six inches since last time we'd met, he must have recognized the horse than me. It seems as though he still towered a foot over me. But I was ten feet tall after that, they all asked "How come the General knows you?" they all asked. I didn't tell them. We saw him again at Yorktown, which turned out to be the big one where we was heading. Last time I spoke to him was at Danbury when he gave me my discharge, I was standing there with my brother, still have my discharge here someplace, but will have to tell you about that another time. The General had a look about him you don't forget, there's hardly any words to describe him. Those were hard days for the most part but there was some good things about them too.[11]

The sequence of events related here is quite impossible, for the army's passage through Head of Elk occurred less than a year after Cook enlisted. If we accept that the elderly veteran lost track of when each of his encounters with Washington occurred, then there is nothing to doubt in these stories except the timeline; they are consistent with what is known of Washington's affability as

11. This passage was recorded by a great-grandson, Frank W. Cook; the date that it was written is unknown. It remains in possession of the family and is used here with the gracious permission of Mr. Burr Cook. Frank W. Cook's preamble reads, "As a young lad I had an opportunity none will have again. We, the Cook kids who grew up at Clarendon were told about the Revolutionary War by its last soldier, our Great Grandfather, Lemuel Cook, who we more affectionately called grampa Lem. He would delight in telling us about his life and we were glad to listen. We'd watch for Lemuel to come out and sit in his rocker either on his front porch or under the big old elm tree in the front yard, as he always did on warm summer afternoons. We would watch for him to motion us to come over with his cane, he always knew we were watching and would run to see who would get there first for the best seat. It would usually start with a question. Tell us about George Washington, what did he look like? He would say 'let me think on it,' a gleam would come to his eye and he would begin to speak slowly and deliberately."

well as his keen interest in horses. It bears noting, though, that the great-grandchild who wrote this tract did so long after he himself had heard the stories, and may have homogenized many of his progenitor's retellings.

After the British capitulation at Yorktown in October 1781, Cook returned to the New York area and rejoined his regiment. There were no more campaigns, no more major battles, but the war was far from over for the 2nd Dragoons. Cook, in his recollections above, mentions that his work "was with Major Tallmadge," but there is no evidence that he participated in any of that officer's intelligence gathering or raiding activities. He may mean simply that he was in the same regiment, given Tallmadge's fame as leader of the Culper spy ring. But Cook also mentions "being in the quartermasters," the department of the army responsible for procurement and movement of supplies. A fellow dragoon, in his pension deposition, recounted difficult work in that capacity which may have been experienced by Cook as well:

> In the Winter of 1781 the Regiment to which I belong'd being stationed at Greenfield I was deputed by Col. (then Major Tallmage) to procure forage and employ Teams to transport it for the use of the Regt. and while in that service and in the line of my duty (having procured several Team loads of Forage) and the weather being extreme cold, the roads very bad and being overtaken by night several miles distant from our station by reason of the difficulty in passing the Road I found on arriving at my station, that my feet were actually frozen notwithstanding.[12]

The 2nd Dragoons spent all of 1782 and the first half of 1783 on duty in New York and Connecticut, working hard at the plethora of military duties that characterized their service. No member of the regiment is known to have left a detailed description of this late period in the war, but the story is told clearly in regimental orders:[13] posting guards; escorting parties of troops and trains of provisions; maintaining horses, clothing, and equipment; forma-

---

12. Pension deposition of John Andrews, R. 214, Revolutionary War Pensions.
13. Two orderly books for this regiment are known to exist, both pertaining primarily to 1782. Orderly book, Mss A 1103, New England Historical and Genealogical Society; Orderly book, Mss #257, New Jersey Historical Society.

tions and inspections; cutting wood. Each day individual dragoons were assigned to be with duty officers so that they were available to carry information when needed; others were assigned to the commander in chief's guard.

The orders reflect the high state of professionalism that the regiment had reached since it was formed in 1776; there was time to refine and standardize procedures such as saluting and other martial niceties. In February 1783 the regiment received musical instruments and planned to form a band consisting of eight "sprightly & active" troopers willing to learn to play them. The army adopted "honorary badges of distinction" awarded to men who had served "with bravery, fidelity and good conduct" for at least three years. The badges were in the form of chevrons ("a narrow piece of cloth in an angular form") applied to coat sleeves, one denoting three years of distinguished service and two denoting six years. A special Badge of Military Merit, forerunner of the Purple Heart medal, was instituted and awarded to a few men in the Continental Army including Sergeant Elijah Churchill of the 2nd Dragoons.[14] We can only wonder if Lemuel Cook attended the presentation ceremony on May 3, 1783.

The chevrons for long and faithful service could be forfeited if a soldier ran afoul of military justice. Men found guilty of military crimes were stripped of these awards; noncommissioned officers were reduced back to private soldiers as well. Regimental courts consisting of several regimental officers were held frequently to try soldiers for misdemeanors such as losing or selling articles of clothing and equipment, damaging ammunition, being absent from roll call or guard duty, being outside camp without a pass, drunkenness, neglect of duty, stealing fowl, livestock, or produce from local residents, insolence toward superiors, disobedience of orders and other crimes. Those found guilty received harsh punishments designed as a warning to others; men of the regiment not occupied with other duties were required to witness the corporal punishments. Lashes, usually twenty-five or fifty, sometimes as many as

---

14. Elijah Churchill's badge of merit is owned by New Windsor Cantonment in New York. *The Legacy of the Purple Heart* (Paducah, KY: Turner Publishing, 2001), 2:20.

one hundred, were applied to the offender's bare back.[15] Other offenders were required to stand barefoot for several minutes on a sharp picket. The gauntlet was particularly galling in that the entire regiment participated in punishing the guilty soldier; the regiment formed two lines, and the offender walked between them, sometimes back and forth several times, with a bayonet held to his breast while each man he passed struck him (the orderly book entries prescribing this punishment do not state whether he was to be struck with sticks, musket ramrods, the flat of sword or bayonet blades, or in some other specific way). These punishments were brutal, but it was an era when corporal punishments were a fact of civilian life as well; dozens of punishments like these were inflicted in the 2nd Dragoons in 1782 and 1783, but the men punished were only a small portion of the several hundred in the regiment. Young Lemuel Cook certainly watched some of his fellows receive these sentences and probably took his swings at a few as part of gauntlets, but he makes no mention of this part of army life and there is no evidence that he himself ever stood trial.

Cleanliness and hygiene are emphasized in general and regimental orders. Although specific means of disease transmission were not known, the correlation between filth and illness was well understood, as was contagion; directions for soldiers to be "neat and clean" were not simply for appearance but for the health and safety of the army. One scourge of the era's armies was smallpox: sometimes fatal but usually survivable, with its rapid transmission the virus could incapacitate large populations for long periods. Even though the practice was controversial, armies often chose to inoculate rather than risk contagion. Smallpox strikes a person only once, after which the victim (if still alive) is immune. Inoculation was accomplished by infecting a person with a small amount of the disease, taken from the sores of another sufferer, and

15. The orderly books from which this information is drawn tell the number of lashes sentenced, but not the extent to which the punishment was carried out. In British regiments, where courts tended to sentence greater numbers of lashes, part or all of the punishment was often remitted, that is, pardoned. Arthur N. Gilbert, "The Regimental Courts Martial in the Eighteenth Century British Army," *Albion: A Quarterly Journal Concerned with British Studies*, 8, no. 1 (Spring 1976), 50–66.

allowing the recipient to recover naturally in controlled conditions, after which he or she was immune to smallpox for life. It was risky; inoculation meant deliberately incapacitating a portion of the army while the disease took hold and then subsided, a period of weeks, but at least the timing could be chosen. It was better than an unpredictable and uncontrolled outbreak. In the early months of 1782, soldiers of the 2nd Dragoons including Lemuel Cook were inoculated, rendering a substantial portion of the regiment unfit for service while they recovered. But they did recover, in time for the new campaign season in late spring.[16]

Winter brought a reduction in activities. The regiment moved from encampments at posts near the front lines in New York and Connecticut into quarters in Connecticut towns. Many soldiers were granted furloughs–long-term leave that allowed them to return home for a designated period, but with the stipulation of returning by a specified date or being punished. During these furloughs some soldiers got married, particularly during the winter of 1782–1783 when the end of the war was imminent.[17] Lemuel Cook makes no mention of having had a furlough, but his discussion of military routine is sparse and no comprehensive records of furloughs survive. Only a few muster rolls survive for the years during which he was a dragoon, and each one indicates that he was present with the regiment for the period covered by the roll.

The year 1783 began with the same routine as the previous one, men returning from furlough, cavalry troops preparing to leave winter quarters, preparations for another season in the field. Then, in April, word came that hostilities had officially ended. There was no more vigilance required, no posts to guard, no threats to reconnoiter. Much work remained, but it could be done at a lighter, easier pace. More men took leave and got married. Wives and rela-

16. The February 1782 muster roll for Captain Staunton's troop lists at least 25 men "under enoculation" including Lemuel Cook, out of 43 altogether; burn damage to the document has destroyed portions of it, making it impossible to see whether some of the individuals were "under enoculation." Another troop had 30 men "in small pox" out of 64 total. Returns and muster rolls, 2nd Light Dragoons, New York State Library.

17. See, for example, the pension depositions of Samuel Grannis, W. 26154, and Michael Couney, W. 16919, Revolutionary War Pensions.

tives visited the camps. In June, the soldiers of the 2nd Dragoons were discharged and sent home, Lemuel Cook among them. Each man received a discharge document, a printed form with his name written in, signed by his commanding officer, stating that he was legally released from his service obligation. Cook's is not known to survive, but was still in his possession when Rev. Hillard interviewed him in 1864. Many others are among the pension records in the National Archives, some indicating that their bearers had received the Badge of Merit for three or six years of service; Cook told Rev. Hillard that his discharge indicated that he had received the Badge of Merit even though he had not completed a full three years. Perhaps his service in 1780, even though for only a few weeks, or the half-year of 1783, was considered enough for him to qualify for the bedge.

The remainder of Lemuel Cook's life is chronicled by Rev. Hillard. He moved from Connecticut to western New York where he spent the remainder of his years, seeing the region evolve from a frontier to a pleasant rural area. He was apparently well known and respected in the community that came to include a large extended family. Friends and family members loved to hear him talk of his experiences in the war, but his celebrity remained strictly local until it became widely known that he was among the last survivors of the American Revolution. That brought him many visitors in his final years, one of whom wrote on January 2, 1865, "Mr. Cook rides out occasionally, and still writes his name quite legibly. He thinks it a little singular, however, that he should be obliged to take an oath of allegiance–swear that he has not given aid and comfort to rebels–whenever he makes application for his pension."[18] The writer apparently refers to protocol required during the Civil War each time Cook went to collect his pension payment. A descendant, writing a century after Cook's death, described the man in his late years; although he did not know Cook personally, he may well have heard these stories directly from family members who did:

> Our revolutionary ancestor, Lemuel Cook, lived to be 107 years of age. He did not die until after the Civil War. He was a

18. Letter to the editor, *New York Herald,* January 2, 1865.

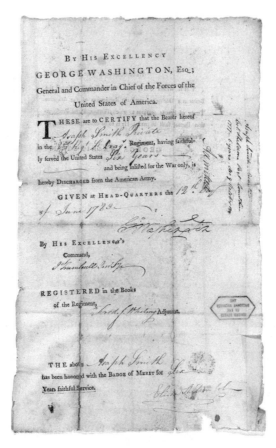

Discharge of Asaph Smith, 2nd Dragoons, prepared on June 12, 1783, and signed by General Washington; Lemuel Cook received an identical document in his name. (*National Archives*)

heavy smoker of cigarettes and cigars. He chewed tobacco. He used snuff. When the old man was 105 years of age he drove from his farm to the village of Clarendon, Orleans County, New York, on Decoration Day. Many of his descendants lived in the town of Clarendon, a crossroads community with one store.

As part of the holiday's celebration in this village, old Lemuel Cook took on his sons, grandsons and great grandsons in wrestling matches and threw them all. The writer's father has told him that the old fellow's descendants cooperated in seeing that the old fellow always won each wrestling match.

Here is an old fellow, a heavy smoker of cigarettes and cigars who at the age of 107 years had not acquired lung cancer. He died because he had just worn out.[19]

Lemuel Cook died on May 20, 1866. He had outlived the other pensioners originally reported as being the last survivors of the Revolution, but by that time some others had been discovered (as described in the Epilogue). Nonetheless, his passing was reported in newspapers all over the country. Most of the obituary notices gave his age as 102, which is probably right given his probable age of 16 when he enlisted in 1780, but some notices say he was 104. One newspaper related that he "spent the last years of his life in a quiet, unostentatious manner, surrounded by his children and grandchildren to the fifth generation. He was plain and frugal in his habits and, possessing an iron constitution, enjoyed good health until within a few months of his death, when he declined into help-less dotage."[20] His funeral was described as follows:

> The funeral of Mr. Cook was held on the 23d day of May, in a beautiful grove about a mile from his residence, under the direction of the Masonic Fraternity, of which he was a member. His remains were followed by a long procession of people from the surrounding Country and from Brockport, Holley, Albion and other villages. Four generations of the patriarch's family–great-great-great-grandchildren–were represented in the group of mourners at the funeral.
>
> Rev. James M. Fuller, of the Methodist Episcopal Church, delivered a very eloquent and appropriate oration on the occasion.[21]
>
> The remains of Mr. Cook were buried in a retired country church-yard in the south east part of the town of Clarendon, N.Y. The Commissioners of Mt. Albion Cemetery–one of the

19. This passage is from a trade journal article asserting that grocers should demand proof that cigarettes cause cancer rather than relying strictly on statistical correlation; it was published when the hazards of smoking were first becoming mainstream knowledge, and warned of decreased profits for grocers if cigarette sales declined. Gordon Cook, "Cigarettes and Cancer," *Voluntary and Cooperative Groups* magazine, New York, NY, December 1969; viewed at tobaccodocuments.org, January 2014.

20. *Frank Leslie's Illustrated Newspaper*, New York, June 16, 1866, 196.

21. Here the account gives the full text of the Psalm 44:1–3.

most beautiful resting places for the dead in the country–of Albion, N.Y., offered a place of burial for him, and the time may come when the offer will be accepted and when Congress or the public will erect some suitable memorial to mark the resting place of the last full-pay Pensioner of the Army of the Revolution.[22]

As with the other pensioners, Rev. Hillard either made no attempt to examine Cook's pension file or inexplicably chose to ignore the contents. The documents reveal that Cook ran into some difficulties with the pension office. In 1790 he received 100 acres of land as a reward for his service and settled in Pompey, Onondaga County, New York. He applied for and received a pension in 1818. In 1820 he followed the requirements of a revision to the pension act and filed a new claim for continuance of his pension. But the intent of this pension act was to accommodate veterans in financial need. In August 1823, Pompey residents contacted the pension office and informed them that Cook was "generally convicted in public Estimation of having made a fraudulent representation of his poverty on or about the 1 Sep 1820 to obtain a continuance of his pension" because he had "within a year or a year & a half sold a farm of which he had been many years in possession in this town & has removed to the western part of this state." The following month his pension was suspended; in the meantime, he resettled farther west in Genesee County. In 1828 a new pension act went into effect that applied to all men who had enlisted in the Continental Army and served until the termination of the war, regardless of current financial need. Lemuel Cook applied for a pension once again and received it, this time for the remainder of his long life.

22. *American Historical Record, and Repertory of Notes and Queries,* Vol. 2, Benson John Lossing, ed. (Philadelphia: Samuel P. Town, 1873), 359.

As a highly visible corps with duties that put its men in close proximity to the Continental army's senior officers, the 2nd Regiment of Light Dragoons was generally well-equipped; in 1781 a French officer described them as "incontestably the best troops on the continent." When sixteen-year-old Lemuel Cook enlisted in the regiment at the end of 1780, it had recently received short green coats with white lapels, cuffs, and collars. While fully serviceable for their duties, these coats were very similar to those worn by some of the loyalist cavalry regiments they were fighting against; this, plus general attempts to standardize the disparate uniforms of the Continental army, may be what caused a change to blue coats with white lapels, cuffs, and collars in 1782.

The regiment ordered brass helmets in 1778, but in 1782 was issued black leather caps with black horsehair crests and mixed red and white plumes. Also in 1778 they were given swords captured from a Brunswick dragoon regiment at the Battle of Bennington the previous year.

The dragoon depicted here wears a white stable jacket with blue cuffs and collar, a utilitarian garment worn for work and leisure. He has tall dragoon boots over long stockings and durable leather breeches. His black leather cap is trimmed with black horsehair, as depicted in a 1782 drawing by a French officer; he holds the heavy Brunswick dragoon sword drawn from the scabbard suspended from its German-style waist-belt.

For more on the clothing of the 2nd Dragoons, see Philip Katcher, *Uniforms of the Continental Army* (York, PA: George Shumway Publisher, 1981), 36; Don Troiani and James Kochan, *Don Troiani's Soldiers of the American Revolution* (Mechanicsburg, PA: Stackpole Books, 2007), 126; H. Charles McBarron and Frederick P. Todd, "2nd Regiment of Continental Light Dragoons, Dismounted Service, 1780," in *Military Uniforms in America: The Era of the American Revolution, 1755–1795* (San Rafael, CA: Presidio Press, 1974), 94–95; Marko Zlatich, *General Washington's Army* (London: Osprey, 1995), 2:12; and 2nd Regiment of Light Dragoons, Revolutionary War Rolls, National Archives and Records Administration

Drawing by Eric H. Schnitzer

The Pension Depositions of Lemuel Cook[23]

1818

State of New York

Onondaga County. On this fifth day of May 1818 before me Sylvanus Tousley one of the judges of the Court of Common pleas for said county personally appears Lemuel Cook aged fifty two years a resident of Pompey in said County and being by me first duly sworn doth on his oath make the following declarations in order to obtain the pension of the late act of Congress entitled "an act to provide for certain persons engaged in the land and naval service of the United States in the revolutionary war. That he the said Lemuel Cook enlisted at Hatfield in Massachusetts in the fore part of the year 1781 to serve during the war and joined the second regiment of light Dragoons commanded by Colonel Shelden, but was mustered in Captain Stantons Company of Infantry, and that he continued to serve in said Corps and in the service of the United States till the month of June 1783 when he was discharged at Danbury in Connecticut. That he has no other evidences now in his possession of his said services and that he is in distressed circumstances and needs the assistance of his country for support.

Sworn to & declared before me the day & year above written.

Lemuel Cook.

1820

[printed form with personal details written in; printed portions in italics]

State of New-York, Onondaga County.

On the first *day of* September *1820, personally appeared in open court in the court of common pleas in and for the county of Onondaga, being a court of record proceeding according to the course of the common law, with a jurisdiction unlimited in point of amount, and keeping a record of their proceedings,* Lemuel Cook *aged* fifty five *years, resident in* Pompey *in said county, who, being first duly sworn according to law, doth on his* oath *declare that he served in the Revolutionary War as fol-*

---

23. Pension deposition of Lemuel Cook, S. 33258, Revolutionary War Pensions.

lows: for two years & six months, from December 1780 to June
1783; he enlisted to serve during the war in Colonel Sheldon's
Regiment of light Dragoons in Captain Stanton's company of light
infantry and continued to serve in said corps during the whole
term and was regularly discharged, that he made his original application or declaration to obtain a pension on the fifth day of May
1818 & has received a pension Certificate No 3120 dated the 25th
September 1818 *and I do solemnly* swear *that I was a resident citizen
of the United States on the 18 day of March, 1818; and that I have not
since that time, by gift, sale, or in any manner, disposed of my property,
or any part thereof, with intent thereby to diminish it, as to bring myself
within the provisions of an act of Congress entitled "An act to provide for
certain persons engaged in the land and naval service of the United
States, in the Revolutionary War," passed on the 18th day of March,
1818; and that I have not, nor has any person in trust for me, any property* necessary wearing apparel & bedding excepted *or securities, contracts, or debts, due to me; nor have I any income other than what is contained in the Schedule hereto annexed, and by me subscribed.*

1 Chest		1.50	1 tea pot	.19	1 spider	.50
1 table		1.00	1 pot 1 kettle	2.00	1 Butcher knife	.25
4 chairs		1.50	1 tea kettle	.25	1 pitcher	.6
1/2 set knives & forks	.50		1 chamber	.25	1 gallon Bottle	.50
1 axe		.50	4 milk pans	.75	1 barrel & Pork	
2 hoes		1.00	2 pails	1.00	say 50 pounds	3.50
1 scythe		.75		12.18	1 cutter	3.00
1/2 set teas & saucers	.12		1 brass kettle	4.00	4 old barrels	.25
6 plates		.37			Cash	.75
						$24.99

& the said Lemuel Cook on his oath aforesaid saith that his
family consists of his wife named Hannah Cook aged fifty two
years, his daughter Hannah Cook aged twelve years, his son
Gilbert Cook aged ten years & his son Selah Cook aged seven
years, that he is by occupation a farmer and in consequence of a
Rupture received in the Revolutionary war, is unable to endure
hard labor, that his wife is worn out with hard labor & unable to
work & that his children are unable to support themselves and are
all constantly resident with him & depend on him for support.

1828

For the purpose of obtaining the benefits of the act entitled an act for the Relief of certain surviving officers & soldiers of the army of the Revolution approved on the 15th of May 1828, I Lemuel Cook of Bergen in the County of Genesee in the state of New York do hereby declare that I enlisted in the Continental Line of the army of the Revolution for and during the war and continued in its service until its termination & during that period I was a private in Captain Stanton's Company in Col. Sheldon's Regiment of Light Dragoons of the line, and I also declare that I have no recollection now that I ever received certificates for the reward of eighty Dollars to which I was entitled under a Resolve of Congress passed the 15th of May 1778. And I further Declare that I was not on the 15th of May 1828 on the Pension list of the United States. I was on the pension list for about two years & my pension stopped about five or six years ago on the ground as I was informed from the War Department that my circumstances were not sufficiently indigent. Witness my hand this twenty seventh day of June in the year of our Lord one thousand eight hundred & twenty eight.

Lemuel Cook.

RESIDENCE of LEMUEL COOK.

LITH. OF BINGHAM & DODD, HARTFORD, CT.

Lithograph of Lemuel Cook's home, Summer 1864, from *Last Men of the Revolution*. (*Society of the Cincinnati*)

Lemuel Cook

From E. B. Hillard, *The Last Men of the Revolution* (1864)

FROM THE HOME OF MR. WALDO, THE MOST DISTINGUISHED, I passed to that of Lemuel Cook, the oldest survivor of the Revolution. He lives in the town of Clarendon, (near Rochester,) Orleans county, New York. His age is one hundred and five years.

Mr. Cook was born in Northbury, Litchfield county, Connecticut, September 10, 1759.[24] He enlisted at Cheshire, in that state, when only sixteen years old. He was mustered in "at Northampton, in the Bay State, 2nd Regiment, Light Dragoons; Sheldon, Col.; Stanton, Capt." He served through the war, and was discharged in Danbury, June 12, 1784.[25] The circumstances of his enlistment and early service he relates as follows:

"When I applied to enlist, Captain Hallibud[26] told me I was so small he couldn't take me unless I would enlist for the war. The first time I smelt gunpowder was at Valentine's Hill (West Chester, New York). A troop of British horse were coming. 'Mount your horses in a minute,' cried the colonel. I was on mine as quick as a squirrel. There were two fires—crash![27] Up came Darrow,[28] good old soul! and said, 'Lem, what do you think of gunpowder? Smell good to you?'

24. As discussed above, Cook was almost certainly born in 1764, because he enlisted in 1780 at the age of sixteen.

25. Actually 1783.

26. Captain George Hurlbut of the 2nd Dragoons. Francis B. Heitman, *Historical Register of Officers of the Continental Army during the War of the Revolution* (Washington, DC: Rare Book Shop Publishing, 1914), 311.

27. "Two fires," that is, two volleys of gunfire.

28. Ebenezer Darrow enlisted in the 2nd Dragoons on April 1, 1777, and served for the remainder of the war. Pension deposition of Ebenezer Darrow, S. 15072, Revolutionary War Pensions.

"The first time I was ordered on sentry was at Dobbs' Ferry. A man came out of a barn and leveled his piece and fired. I felt the wind of the ball. A soldier near me said, 'Lem, they mean you; go on the other side of the road.' So I went over; and pretty soon another man came out of the barn and aimed and fired. He didn't come near me. Soon another came out and fired. His ball lodged in my hat. By this time the firing had roused the camp; and a company of our troops came on one side, and a party of the French on the other; and they took the men in the barn prisoners, and brought them in. They were Cow Boys.[29] This was the first time I saw the French in operation. They stepped as though on edge.[30] They were a dreadful proud nation. When they brought the men in, one of them had the impudence to ask, 'Is the man here we fired at just now?' 'Yes,' said Major Tallmadge, 'there he is, that boy.' Then he told how they had each laid out a crown, and agreed that the one who brought me down should have the three. When he got through with his story, I stepped to my holster and took out my pistol,[31] and walked up to him and said, 'If I've been a mark to you for money, I'll take my turn now. So, deliver your money, or your life!' He handed over four crowns, and I got three more from the other two."[32]

Mr. Cook was at the battle of Brandywine[33] and at Cornwallis' surrender. Of the latter he gives the following account:

"It was reported Washington was going to storm New York. We had made a by-law in our regiment that every man should stick to his horse: if his horse went, he should go with him. I was waiter for the quartermaster;[34] and so had a chance to keep my horse in good

29. Cowboys, the sobriquet given to loyalist cavalry operating in Westchester County.

30. Stepped as if on edge, that is, the French marched in a light and careful manner.

31. Dragoon pistols were carried in holsters that strapped to the saddle, so Cook had to go to his saddle to get a pistol.

32. No other account of this capture of three loyalists has been found, but tussles between the two sides were common in this region.

33. Cook clearly was not at the Battle of Brandywine on September 11, 1777; Hillard may have confused this with the little-known battle at Valentine's Hill in July 1781.

34. Waiter, a servant to an officer. This was a common duty for young soldiers.

condition. Baron Steuben was mustermaster.[35] He had us called out to select men and horses fit for service. When he came to me he said, 'Young man, how old are you?' I told him. 'Be on the ground to-morrow morning at nine o'clock,' said he. My colonel didn't like to have me go. 'You'll see,' said he 'they'll call for him to-morrow morning.' But they said if we had a law, we must abide by it. Next morning, old Steuben had got my name. There were eighteen out of the regiment. 'Be on the ground,' said he, 'to-morrow morning with two days' provisions.' 'You're a fool,' said the rest; 'they're going to storm New York.' No more idea of it than of going to Flanders.[36] My horse was a bay, and pretty. Next morning I was the second on parade. We marched off towards White Plains. Then, 'left wheel,'[37] and struck right north. Got to King's Ferry, below Tarrytown. There were boats, scows, &c. We went right across into the Jerseys. That night I stood with my back to a tree.[38] Then we went on to the head of Elk. There the French were. It was dusty; 'peared to me I should have choked to death. One of 'em handed me his canteen; 'Lem,' said he, 'take a good horn we're going to march all night.'[39] I didn't know what it was, so I took a full drink. It liked to have strangled me. Then we were in Virginia. There wasn't much fighting. Cornwallis tried to force his way north to New York; but fell into the arms of La Fayette, and he drove him back.[40] Old Rochambeau told 'em, 'I'll land five hundred

35. General Friedrich von Steuben was the Inspector General of the Continental army, effectively the same as a muster master, but he was not with Washington's army at this time; he had gone south to serve with General Nathanael Greene, and then had taken leave due to illness during the summer of 1781. Cook may have encountered von Steuben at some point, but this incident certainly involved a different officer. For von Steuben's career see Paul Douglas Lockhart, *The Drillmaster of Valley Forge: The Baron de Steuben and the Making of the American Army* (New York: HarperCollins, 2008).

36. That is, Cook's fellow soldiers thought Cook would be killed in an attack on New York, but Cook was naïve about the danger.

37. Left wheel, the command for turning a line of soldiers on the march.

38. That is, he slept standing up, leaning on a tree.

39. A good horn, that is, a good long drink; even though military canteens were typically tin or wood, the expression refers to drinking from a horn cup.

40. The British army did make an attempt to escape by crossing the York River but were thwarted by bad weather; had they succeeded in crossing, they would have had to break through forces commanded by General Lafayette.

from the fleet, against your eight hundred.'[41] But they darsn't. We were on a kind of a side hill. We had plaguey little to eat and nothing to drink under heaven. We hove up some brush to keep the flies off.[42] Washington ordered that there should be no laughing at the British; said it was bad enough to have to surrender without being insulted. The army came out with guns clubbed on their backs.[43] They were paraded on a great smooth lot, and there they stacked their arms. Then came the devil—old women, and all (camp followers).[44] One said, 'I wonder if the d———d Yankees will give me any bread.' The horses were starved out. Washington turned out with his horses and helped 'em up the hill. When they see the artillery, they said, 'there, them's the very artillery that belonged to Burgoyne.'[45] Greene came from the southward; the awfullest set you ever see.[46] Some, I should presume, had a pint of lice on 'em. No boots nor shoes."

The old man's talk is very broken and fragmentary. He recalls the past slowly, and with difficulty; but when he has fixed his mind upon it, all seems to come up clear. His articulation, also, is very imperfect; so that it is with difficulty that his story can be made out. Much of his experience in the war seems gone from him; and in conversation with him he has to be left to the course of his own thoughts, inquiries and suggestions appearing to confuse him. At the close of the war, he married Hannah Curtis, of Cheshire, Connecticut; and lived a while in that vicinity; after which he

41. It is not clear what Cook means by this, except perhaps to say that Rochambeau considered French troops superior to those of the British.

42. It was very common during the war for soldiers to be without tents, and to build shelters out of brush instead. See John U. Rees, "'We . . . Got Ourselves Cleverly Settled for the Night. . .': Soldiers' Shelter on Campaign During the War for Independence," *Military Collector & Historian*, 55:2 (Summer 2003), 89–96.

43. Guns clubbed, that is, muskets held with the butt upward and the muzzle down, a sign of surrender.

44. Camp followers, the wives and families of soldiers and other dependents and refugees.

45. When General Burgoyne's army surrendered at Saratoga in October 1777, its artillery fell into American hands; some of these guns were at Yorktown, and some British soldiers who had escaped captivity were serving in Cornwallis's army.

46. That is, the army under Major General Nathanael Greene which had been operating in South Carolina and was poorly supplied with clothing.

removed to Utica, New York. There he had frequent encounters with the Indians who still infested the region. One with whom he had some difficulty about cattle, at one time assailed him at a public house, as he was on his way home, coming at him with great fury, with a drawn knife. Mr. Cook was unarmed; but catching up a chair he presented it as a shield against the Indian's thrusts, till help appeared. He says he never knew what fear was, and always declared that no man should take him prisoner alive. His frame is large, his presence commanding; and in his prime he must have possessed prodigious strength. He has evidently been a man of most resolute spirit; the old determination still manifesting itself in his look and words. His voice, the full power of which he still retains, is marvellous for its volume and strength. Speaking of the present war, he said, in his strong tones, at the same time bringing down his cane with force upon the floor, "It is terrible; but, terrible as it is, *the rebellion must be put down!*" He still walks comfortably with the help of a cane; and with the aid of glasses reads his "book," as he calls the Bible. He is fond of company, loves a joke, and is good-natured in a rough sort of way. He likes to relate his experiences in the army and among the Indians. He has voted the Democratic ticket since the organization of the government, supposing that it still represents the same party that it did in Jefferson's time. His pension, before its increase, was one hundred dollars. It is now two hundred dollars. The old man's health is comfortably good; and he enjoys life as much as could be expected at his great age. His home, at present, is with a son, whose wife, especially, seems to take kind and tender care of him. Altogether, he is a noble old man; and long may it yet be before his name shall be missed from the roll of his country's deliverers.

Lemuel Cook, photographed by Messrs. N. A. and R. A. Moore, 1864.
(*Society of the Cincinnati*)

4

Alexander Milliner

1st New York Regiment

IN EACH VETERAN'S STORY RELATED BY REV. HILLARD THERE ARE factual errors of the sort that can be attributed to the fading memories of aged men. It is clear that Rev. Hillard did little or no research to corroborate the stories he heard, instead accepting them as fact regardless of apparent discrepancies. In most cases he can be excused for this: his work had a clear purpose, and it was not as a history book but as a memorial. The book was a monument not to young men serving in the American Revolution but to the centenarians who had survived for so long.

In spite of this caveat, it is difficult to accept Rev. Hillard's memoir of Alexander Milliner. From the first paragraph, it contains inaccuracies so blatant that it is hard to imagine how they could have been accepted at face value. And yet that is what was done by Rev. Hillard and generations of historians who followed, propagating a life not just misremembered but in many ways impossible. In at least one case Rev. Hillard discounted factual information from a credible source in favor of what he had learned during his visit with Milliner. Perhaps it was out of reverence for the veterans who had witnessed the nation's birth, or perhaps it simply suited his purpose. Like the other soldiers' chronicles, though, after the facts are separated from the fiction there remains a fine story, one that deserves telling and that may have more in common with the old man's clouded recollections than is initially apparent.

The first discrepancy is the most blatant and lays the foundation of doubt about what follows. Although he does not quote Milliner directly, Rev. Hillard claims that Milliner was born in March 1760, putting the veteran's age at 104 when he visited Milliner in 1864. This would not be implausible in and of itself; a man born that year was an ideal age to be a soldier in the American Revolution. But Milliner was not an ordinary soldier; the cachet of his service is that he was a drummer boy, an iconic figure of the war, too young to tote a musket but determined to beat a drum for his country. And yet, just one sentence after giving Milliner's age, Rev. Hillard

wrote that he was "too young at the time of his enlistment for service in the ranks." Were the age of 104 correct, Milliner would have
reached 16 years of age in 1776.

Not all drummers of the era were boys; many adults played that
instrument for the army well into middle age, training and tutoring
the young ones.[1] Milliner's own words, though, dwell on the fact
of his youth when he was in the army. Rev. Hillard wrote that
General Washington would "come along and pat him on the head,
and call him his boy," something difficult to imagine had Milliner
been 16 in 1776 and 23 when the army disbanded in 1783.
Milliner's own pension deposition in 1819 gives an age that correlates to birth in 1770, and fellow pension applicants corroborated
that date; sources contemporary to Rev. Hillard's book also agree
with this date.[2] Oddly enough, Rev. Hillard mentions this information and then declares it inaccurate without indicating whether his
own source for the 1760 date was Milliner himself or others. The
contradiction of the "drummer boy" born in 1760 has been repeated ever since it was first published. As will be seen below, the 1770
date is certainly correct.

Rev. Hillard relates that Milliner's father was a goldsmith who
came with his wife to America with the British army during the
French and Indian War; with his son still in the womb, he died
while participating in the British capture of Quebec in 1759. No
record of a goldsmith by the name of Milliner has been found,[3] but
that is not what makes the tale implausible; tradesmen often joined
the British army as artificers and as soldiers soon after, or even
before, finishing their apprenticeships; wives often accompanied
the army on overseas service. For this story to be true, though,
Milliner would have had to have been born in 1760. The elder

1. John U. Rees, "'The Music of the Army': An Abbreviated Study of the Ages
of Musicians in the Continental Army," *Brigade Dispatch* 24:4 (Autumn 1994),
2–8.

2. Most notably the pension office letter of February 18, 1864, that was widely published and led to the congressional resolution of thanks on March 4, 1864.

3. Wendell D. Garrett, ed., *The Last Men of the Revolution* (Barre, MA: Barre
Publishers, 1968), 68; this book is an annotated revision of the 1864 edition.

Milliner may have been in British military employ in Quebec when he died, but he certainly remained alive until 1769 or 1770.[4]

That Milliner's mother married a man named Florence Maroney is apparently true. No marriage records have been found, but Milliner's pension deposition and corroborating statements indicate that Milliner was enlisted into the army by his father, Florence Maroney, who was a soldier in the 1st New York Regiment. Maroney enlisted for the duration of the war on November 28, 1776, and was immediately appointed sergeant.[5] This rank may have been awarded based on prior military service, in recognition of organizational skills, as a reward for having enlisted other men, or simply as a favor from an officer with whom he was well acquainted. The fact that Maroney retained this rank for the remainder of the war shows that it was well-deserved, and his signatures on many military documents testify not only to his literacy but to his abilities in discharging the duties of his office.[6] Around the time the regiment marched from Fort Schuyler in the Mohawk River valley to West Point on the Hudson River, he enlisted his stepson Alexander into the regiment as a drummer.

During his youth, Alexander Milliner used his stepfather's family name; military documents show him as Alexander Maroney. He applied for a pension under the latter name in 1819, a sensible choice to ensure that his application correlated with available records. A muster roll of Captain Nicholas Van Rensselaer's company of the 1st New York Regiment shows that Alexander Milliner, under the name Alexander Maroney, enlisted on

4. No rolls of British military artificers from this era are known to exist. Muster rolls for some of the British regiments serving in Canada at this time are available but were not searched for this study, because the absence of a soldier named Milliner would not disprove a connection with the army.

5. T. W. Egly, Jr., *History of the First New York Regiment 1775–1783* (Hampton, NH: Peter E. Randall, 1981), 289.

6. A number of pay receipts for Captain Jansen's company of the 1st New York Regiment are signed by Florence Maroney, and bear his name as witness to each soldier's signature. Muster rolls, 1st New York Regiment (1777–1783), Revolutionary War Rolls, New York.

September 1, 1780, and "joined" on October 15 of that year.[7] This suggests that the elder Maroney was on some sort of detached service or furlough when he enlisted his son. Milliner stated in his pension deposition that he was enlisted at Lake George, a post manned by detachments from New York regiments. The October 15 date is just a few days after the regiment's arrival at West Point.[8] This correlates with Milliner's 1819 statement that he had served "he thinks three or four years" before being discharged in June 1783; a man who served with him deposed that Milliner served "three years and one half or thereabout."[9] This means that Milliner was ten years old when he was put on the regiment's rolls, consistent with his memories of being a drummer boy for his entire service, rather than growing into adulthood during the war, as would have been the case if he had been born in 1760 and enlisted early in the war.

Service from October 1780 through June 1783 does not square with the remarkable battle experience presented by Rev. Hillard. Again not quoting directly, he states that Milliner was at the battle of White Plains in October 1776, Brandywine in September 1777, Saratoga (whether the battle of Freeman's Farm in September, Bemis Heights in October, or the surrender later that month is not stated), Monmouth in June 1778, and Yorktown in October 1781 in addition to service in the Mohawk Valley and presence at the 1778 encampment at Valley Forge. While some soldiers were present at many of the war's premier conflicts, participation in the concurrent campaigns that included both Brandywine and Saratoga is implausible enough that one wonders how Rev. Hillard failed to notice it. The 1st New York Regiment, however, was not involved in either campaign, instead having marched farther west as part of the relief of besieged Fort Schuyler. The regiment did not winter at Valley Forge in 1778, but instead arrived there in May for only a brief stay

7. "A Muster Roll of Capt Nicholas VRensselaers Compy in the first Battalion New York forces in the Service of the United States Commanded by Colonel Goose VSchaack for the Months of Sepr Octor Novr and December 1780." Muster rolls, 1st New York Regiment (1777–1783), Revolutionary War Rolls, New York.

8. Egly, *History of the First New York Regiment,* 169.

9. Pension deposition of Alexander Milliner (filed as Alexander Maroney) including a deposition by Elijah Reynolds, S. 42925, Revolutionary War Pensions.

Detail from the muster roll of Captain Van Rensselaer's company of the 1st New York Regiment; Alexander Maroney is the "Drum" listed left center, with his enlistment date adjacent. (*National Archives*)

before the entire army left that encampment. Even though the regiment was involved in some of the actions mentioned by Rev. Hillard, Alexander Milliner had not yet enlisted when they occurred. He was only six years old when the battle of White Plains was fought. Could an eight-year-old boy have been somehow wounded at the June 1778 battle of Monmouth?

Another discrepancy is Rev. Hillard's claim that Milliner served in the corps called Washington's Life Guard. Milliner makes no mention of this special regiment in his pension depositions, and although he related a vignette concerning the corps to Rev. Hillard, there is no direct quotation from Milliner indicating service in the Life Guard. It seems like much of what Rev. Hillard wrote about

Alexander Milliner, whether related directly by the veteran or inferred by the author, is false. There may be more truth to it, however, than is immediately obvious.

We have seen that the young drummer enlisted under the name of his stepfather, Florence Maroney, who had been in the army since late 1776 when Milliner was six years old. Rev. Hillard says that Milliner's mother, Mrs. Maroney, "accompanied the army as a washerwoman." This is entirely plausible, particularly if we accept that she had originally come to America as an army wife; many wives of American, British, and German soldiers followed their husbands into garrisons and on campaigns.[10] Far from idle impediments, these women earned their keep by supporting the army infrastructure, working as laundresses, hospital nurses, and purveyors of provisions. And sometimes their children accompanied them. Their presence is revealed in the form of numbers on lists and returns, but unfortunately very few of these wives and children are mentioned by name in military records.[11] Although no proof exists, it is entirely plausible that Mrs. Maroney and her young son accompanied Sergeant Maroney on some or all of the 1st New York Regiment's campaigns from the time of Maroney's enlistment in November 1776. If that is the case, many of Milliner's stories may be genuine memories, including recollections of the 1777 siege of Fort Schuyler, better known as Fort Stanwix, and a visit to Valley Forge that included seeing Martha Washington. He may have seen the infamous General Charles Lee and been present at the battle of Monmouth. There is even a chance that he was wounded in that battle, a fate that occasionally befell wives and children who strayed too close to the fighting or had the fighting stray close to them.[12]

10. For a detailed discussion of wives and families in the Continental army see Holly A. Mayer, *Belonging to the Army: Camp Followers and Community During the American Revolution* (Columbia: University of South Carolina Press, 1996); for the British army, see Don N. Hagist, "The Women of the British Army During the American Revolution," *Minerva Quarterly Report on Women and the Military* 13:2 (Summer 1995).

11. For a rare example of a woman's firsthand account of campaigning with a New York regiment, see the narrative of Sarah Osborn in John C. Dann, *The Revolution Remembered: Eyewitness Accounts of the War for Independence* (Chicago: University of Chicago Press, 1980), 240–250.

12. For examples of women being exposed to the dangers of combat, see Hagist, "The Women of the British Army in the American Revolution," 62, 65–67.

Other discrepancies in Milliner's recollections also have plausible explanations. His account of British soldiers surrendering at Saratoga could actually be a memory from Yorktown, an event he did witness. If he told Rev. Hillard he had been at White Plains, he may have referred to his regiment's service in that area near Dobbs Ferry in July and August 1781 rather than the famous October 1776 battle. As for service in the Life Guard, that corps was composed of men selected from other regiments. Complete rolls of the Life Guard are not known to exist; Milliner (under the name of Alexander Maroney) is not among those known to have served in the unit, but he nonetheless may have been in it for some part of his service.[13] In short, some portions of Alexander Milliner's wartime service related by Rev. Hillard that are not congruent with the service of either him or his regiment may nonetheless be based on genuine memories, with details confused either by age or by Rev. Hillard's inaccurate interpretations. It is just as likely, though, that Milliner mixed memories of his own experience with familiar stories repeated throughout the new nation in the years following the war. Eighty years after the fact, it is only natural that his reminiscences of childhood experiences were intertwined with information accumulated from a lifetime of other sources.

Knowing that Alexander Milliner joined his regiment on October 25, 1780, we can chronicle his service from that date onward by following the regiment's activities and assuming that the young drummer was not detached or absent for any significant periods. The 1st New York regiment left West Point in November 1780 and spent the winter in barracks in Albany, always ready to move from that key location in response to threats from the north or west. Detachments manned the nearby posts of Fort Edward and Saratoga. They sent out scouting parties, guarded supply trains, and performed the myriad tasks expected of soldiers in relatively safe but nonetheless important locations. A young drummer probably spent most of his time at the barracks and garrisons, but had a critical role in keeping the military system running smoothly. Drums were used for signaling. The regiment's daily

13. A list of all soldiers known to have served in the Life Guard appears in Carlos Emmor Godfrey, *The Commander in Chief's Guard, Revolutionary War* (Washington, DC: Stevenson-Smith Co., 1904), 113–274.

routine was regulated by distinctive beatings of the drum from reveille in the morning until taptoo at night, with tunes announcing meals, formations, noncommissioned officers call, procurement of firewood, pay call, and all manner of other duties. When the regiment was formed, drum signals conveyed orders for every movement and maneuver; used primarily to train soldiers to handle muskets and march in unison, a subset of signals conveyed critical combat commands such as advance, retreat, and commence and cease firing. These signals were largely standardized in military manuals widely available in Europe and America, taught to individual drummers by the regiment's drum major.[14] If Alexander Milliner did follow the army as a boy he may have been familiar with drum signals when he began performing the role himself; regardless, he was kept busy practicing his musical skills in addition to providing essential communication for the regiment's daily routine.

In the summer of 1781 the 1st New York Regiment joined Washington's army for the journey south that culminated in the British surrender at Yorktown. A hard fifteen-day march through New Jersey to Head of Elk, Maryland, including a proud procession through Philadelphia to beating drums,[15] culminated in embarkation on transport ships for the remainder of the trip to Virginia.[16] It may have been on this campaign that the young drummer first caught the notice of General Washington; it is also quite plausible that he met the British General Cornwallis, as he related to Rev. Hillard. His first year in the army was certainly the most eventful. After taking some time to "level" the no-longer-needed fortifications around Yorktown, the 1st New York Regiment headed north again, arriving at Pompton, New Jersey, where they built huts that would be their homes for the winter and much of the following year. In March 1782 General and Mrs. Washington paid a visit to the Pompton cantonment, perhaps the basis for Milliner's statements that he saw them at Valley Forge.[17]

14. See Raoul F. Camus, *Military Music of the American Revolution* (Chapel Hill: University of North Carolina Press, 1975).

15. James Thacher, *Military Journal of the American Revolution* (Hartford, CT: Hurlbut, Williams & Co., 1862), 271–274.

16. The 1st New York regiment marched on to Annapolis before embarking. Egly, *History of the First New York Regiment*, 202.

17. Egly, *History of the First New York Regiment*, 215.

Even though a large British garrison occupied nearby New York, 1782 was a quiet year for the New York soldiers in the Pompton cantonment. In late August they finally changed stations, moving to an encampment at Verplank's Point on the east side of the Hudson River. In September they ceremoniously greeted their French allies who passed through on their march from the southward.[18] The 1st New York remained militarily vigilant, but no threats came. By the end of October they were on the move again, this time to the Continental Army's final cantonment at New Windsor, New York. Here, during the first half of 1783, Alexander Milliner was again in close proximity to General Washington; if the various anecdotes Milliner related about being a favorite of the great general are true, they most likely took place during these final months of service. Regardless of whether he'd accompanied the army as a boy with his father or had been exposed to the martial environment for the first time when he enlisted in 1780, Milliner had had ample time to learn various ways to entertain his comrades and become "the life of the camp." He also learned the skills of a drummer sufficiently well to impress his peers and retain his abilities for the rest of his life, even though his regiment was consistently short of drums.[19] Milliner and his father were discharged from the army in June 1783.

From the time Milliner left the army as a young teenager until he applied for a pension, little is known of his life. Probably he stayed with his parents for at least a few years, settling on the land grant in Seneca County that Florence Maroney received in 1790. Milliner married in the early nineteenth century, and his first child was born in 1806. By 1819 he had settled in the town of Homer in Courtland County, New York. Among the things he did not do, or at least for which there is no evidence, is serve in the United States Navy during the War of 1812. Rev. Hillard tells of Milliner's service on board the famous frigate U.S.S. *Constitution* during storied naval engagements, but there is no record that he served on that

18. Egly, *History of the First New York Regiment*, 232.

19. Inspection returns show that the regiment had only three drums for nine drummers in June 1782; by April of the following year they had acquired only two more drums. Egly, *History of the First New York Regiment*, 221, 261.

Pay list of the 1st New York Regiment showing Sgt. Florence Maroney's signature by his own name, and as witness to the other signatures. (*National Archives*)

ship or any other.[20] He made no mention of naval service in his 1819 or 1820 pension materials, something that cannot be ascribed to oversight, being only a few years removed from the war. The birth of children in 1812 and 1814 also testify against any long naval career during that era.[21] Perhaps he spent time as a merchant seaman after his Revolutionary War career, and reconfigured his memories of those times later in his life.

Alexander Milliner died on March 13, 1865. He was widely reported to have been 105 years of age, but was actually very close to 95. This discrepancy does not diminish the importance of the veteran who had been a local celebrity in his old age, and who had gained national recognition when the list of surviving pensioners was published. Milliner's story as told by Rev. Hillard was exaggerated and embellished wildly beyond his actual achievements and continues to be propagated in the same manner without discernment. This is a shame, because the true story of his service as a young drummer during desperate days of conflict is remarkable enough, deserving of proper recognition without elaboration.

---

20. Garrett, ed., *The Last Men of the Revolution*, 73.
21. The ages of his children are given in his 1820 pension deposition.

As a young drummer, Alexander Milliner may have had an elaborate, attractive uniform or no uniform at all. Military fashion dictated that drummers wear distinctive uniforms, often with the color of the coat body and the lapels, cuffs, and collar reversed from that of the private soldiers. The constant challenges for each state to actually provide the authorized clothing, however, meant that practical considerations took precedence over style. It was Milliner's good fortune to join the regiment in October 1780 and serve for the remainder of the war, years when the regiment was generally well supplied.

In 1782 the 1st New York received British uniforms captured by the Spanish and donated to the United States. This clothing was probably better made and more elaborate than any they had worn previously. The red coats were disassembled, dyed brown, and then remade with their colorful lapels, cuffs, collars, and buttonhole lace unchanged. The drummer pictured here wears a drummer's coat from the British 55th Regiment of Foot; with reversed colors, that is, a green coat with red lapels, cuffs, and collar; it may not have been dyed like the red coats. Two widths of worsted lace bearing an elaborate geometric design adorn the buttonholes, sleeves, and edges of the coat. His cocked hat is one issued annually to British drummers as an alternative to the bearskin caps used for formal occasions. The drum is hooked to a broad leather strap with loops to hold the drum sticks. A single length of rope is threaded through the wooden hoops holding the drum heads; pushing down on the leather tensioners tightens the rope to get the right sound from the heads.

For more on the clothing of the 1st New York Regiment, see Philip Katcher, *Uniforms of the Continental Army* (York, PA: George Shumway Publisher, 1981), 122; Don Troiani and James Kochan, *Don Troiani's Soldiers of the American Revolution* (Mechanicsburg, PA: Stackpole Books, 2007), 179; and Don Troiani and James Kochan, *Insignia of Independence: Military Buttons, Accoutrement Plates, and Gorgets of the American Revolution* (Gettysburg, PA: Thomas Publications, 2012), 191–192.

Drawing by Eric H. Schnitzer

The Pension Depositions of Alexander Milliner[22]

1819

State of New York, Courtland County

On this fifteenth day of April 1819 before me the subscriber first judge of the court of common pleas in and for the county of Cortland in the state of N York, personally appears Alexander Marony aged forty nine years resident in the town of Homer said county who being by me first duly sworn according to Law doth on his oath make the flowing declaration in order to obtain the provision made by the act of congress passed the 18th day of March 1818 entitled an act to provide for certain persons engaged in the land and naval service of the United States in the revolutionary war that the said Alexander Marony was enlisted by his father Florence Maroney at Lake George in the State of New York as Drummer in the company commanded by Captain Graham and shortly after Captain Graham was appointed Major[23] and he was put under the Command of Captain Johnson[24] in Colo. Vanscaiks[25] regiment in the first New York Regiment in the New York line and served in the same line or service of the United States until June 1783 at the close of the war when he was discharged at Snake Hill back of New Winsor in the state of New York; that his father enlisted him (as he was young) and got his discharge at the close of the war that he cannot tell exactly how long he served but he thinks three or four years that his father died from home and lost all his

22. Pension file of Alexander Milliner (filed as Alexander Maroney, even though the name is spelled Marony in the deposition), S. 42925, Revolutionary War Pensions.

23. Captain John Graham had been appointed major in March 1779 but still commanded a company. Milliner refers to the reorganization of the regiment on January 1, 1781, when Major Graham no longer commanded a company and Captain Cornelius Jansen joined the regiment. This statement by Milliner has led some authors to conclude that he enlisted before March 1779, that is, before Graham was promoted to major. Egly, *History of the First New York Regiment*, 120, 178, 289.

24. Captain Cornelius Jansen. Milliner, under the name of Alexander Maroney, is not on the rolls of Captain Jansen's company but his stepfather, Florence Maroney, is listed.

25. Colonel Goose van Schaick, commander of the 1st New York Regiment.

papers and his discharge with the rest. That he is in reduced circumstances and stands in need of assistance from his country for support. Sworn to and declared before me the day and in the year aforesaid. [signed] Alexander Marony

John Keep First Judge of Cortland Common pleas.

1820

State of New York, Cortland County

On this 12th day of September 1820 personally appeared in Open Court being a Court of Record by the laws of the said state of New York, in the said County of Cortland, called the court of Common pleas, Alexander Marony aged fifty years resident of the town of Homer in the said County of Cortland who being first duly sworn according to law doth on his oath declare that he served in the Revolutionary War as follows: that he enlisted under Capt. Graham, was afterwards assigned to the company commanded by Capt. Johnson in Col. Van Schaicks first New York Regiment on the Continental establishment that he served Three Years & six months and was discharged near Newburgh at a place called Snake Hill in this State that his original declaration bears the date the 15th day of April 1819; and that the pension Certificate issued thereupon is numbered 15,644; and I do solemnly swear that I was a resident citizen of the United States on the 18th day of March 1818 that I have not since that time by gift sale or in any manner disposed of my property, or any part thereof with Intent thereby so to diminish it as to bring myself within the provisions of an act of Congress entitled "an act to provide for certain persons engaged in the land & naval service of the United States in the revolutionary war" passed on the 18th day of March 1818 and that I have not nor has any person in trust for me any property or securities contracts or debts due, to me nor have I any income other than what is contained in the schedule hereto annexed by me subscriber.

Real Estate I have none

1 Calf, 5 pigs, 1 ox yoke 1 plough, 1 drag, 1 chain all worn, 1 good axe, 1 poor axe, 1 sythe, 1 sickle, 1 cow bell, 4 old chairs, 1 old chest, 2 dishkettles, 1 plate, 4 knives & 3 forks old & broken, halfset Tea Cups & Saucers, 2 old pails, 1 meat barrel

Alexander Marony

And the said Alexander Marony further swears that he is by occupation a farmer, that his bodily infirmities render him at times unable to labor that he has a wife Abigail Marony aged forty four years and is & has been for three years sickly, with a slender constitution and unable to perform hard labor, that he has six Children dependant upon him for support to wit: Patty Marony aged fourteen who is of a feeble & slender Constitution & unable to perform ordinary labor, Merriam Marony aged twelve years, Sally Marony aged ten years, Joel P. Potter Marony aged Eight years inclined to insanity & probably will never be able to support himself, John Marony aged six years, Polly Marony aged about two months.

Sworn to & Declard on the 12th day of September 1820 before Edward C. Reed, Barak Niles, Oliver Wiswell, Judges of Cortland com. Plea

RESIDENCE of ALEXANDER MILLENER.

LITH. OF BINGHAM & DODD, HARTFORD, CT.

Lithograph of Alexander Milliner's home, Summer 1864, from *Last Men of the Revolution*. (*Society of the Cincinnati*)

Alexander Milliner

From E. B. Hillard, *The Last Men of the Revolution* (1864)

A FEW MILES FROM MR. COOK, AT ADAM'S BASIN, ON THE Rochester and Niagara Falls division of the Central Railroad, lives Alexander Milliner, fourth of the survivors visited.

Mr. Milliner was born at Quebec on the 14th of March, 1760. His father was an English goldsmith, who came over with Wolfe's army as an artificer, his wife accompanying him. At the scaling of the Heights of Abraham, he was detailed for special service, and at the close of the battle, lying down to drink at a spring on the plain, he never rose again; the cold water, in his heated and exhausted condition, causing instant death.

His widow remained a while at Quebec, where, as has been said, in the following spring Alexander was born. While he was yet young, his mother,—whom her son describes as "English, high larnt, understood all languages, had been a teacher,"—removed with him to New York, where, becoming acquainted with a man by the name of Maroney, a well-to-do mason, she married him. This explains the circumstance of Mr. Milliner's name appearing on the pension roll as "Alexander Maroney;"—his step-father, by whom, on account of his youth, he was enlisted, doing it under his own name. The enlistment, Mr. Milliner says, was at New York; though the record of the Pension Office gives it at Lake George. The pension roll, too, gives ninety-four years as Mr. Milliner's age. This is manifestly an error of ten years; since the battle of Quebec, the fall before his birth, occurred on the 13th of September, 1759. On the 14th of March, of the present year, therefore, Mr. Milliner was one hundred and four years old.

Too young at the time of his enlistment for service in the ranks, he was enlisted as drummer boy; and in this capacity he served four years, in Washington's Life Guard. He was a great favorite, he says, with the Commander-in-Chief, who used frequently, after the beating of the reveille, to come along and pat him on the head, and call him his boy. On one occasion, "a bitter cold morning," he gave him a drink out of his flask. His recollection of Washington is distinct and vivid: "He was a good man, a beautiful man. He was always pleasant; never changed countenance, but wore the same in defeat and retreat as in victory." Lady Washington, too, he recollects, on her visits to the camp. "She was a short, thick woman; very pleasant and kind. She used to visit the hospitals, was kindhearted, and had a motherly care. One day the General had been out some time. When he came in, his wife asked him where he had been. He answered, laughing, 'to look at my boys.' 'Well,' said she, 'I will go and see *my* children.' When she returned, the General inquired, 'What do you think of them?' 'I think,' answered she, 'that there are a good many.' They took a great notion to me. One day the General sent for me to come up to headquarters. 'tell him,' he sent word, 'that he needn't fetch his drum with him.' I was glad of that. The Life Guard came out and paraded, and the roll was called. There was one Englishman, Bill Dorchester. The General said to him, 'Come, Bill, play up this 'ere Yorkshire tune.' When he got through, the General told me to play. So I took the drum, overhauled her, braced her up,[26] and played a tune. The General put his hand in his pocket and gave me three dollars; then one and another gave me more—so I made out well; in all, I got fifteen dollars. I was glad of it: my mother wanted some tea, and I got the poor old woman some." His mother accompanied the army as washerwoman, for the sake of being near her boy.

He relates the following anecdote of General Washington:

"We were going along one day, slow march, and came to where the boys were jerking stones.[27] 'Halt' came the command. 'Now,

26. Milliner refers to the process of adjusting the drum heads to his satisfaction. Drum heads were held tight by rope braces on the sides of the drum; adjusting the tension of the ropes tightened or loosened the head, changing the sound. A skilled drummer could "overhaul and brace" a rope-tensioned drum very quickly.

27. Jerk: "To throw with a quick, smart motion; as, to jerk a stone. We apply this word to express the mode of throwing to a little distance by drawing the arm back of the body, and thrusting it forward against the side or hip, which stops the arm suddenly." Noah Webster, *An American Dictionary of the English Language* (New York: S. Converse, 1828).

boys,' said the General, 'I will show you how to jerk a stone.' He beat 'em all. He smiled, but didn't laugh out."

Mr. Milliner was at the battles of White Plains, Brandywine, Saratoga, Monmouth, Yorktown, and some others. The first of these he describes as "a nasty battle." At Monmouth he received a flesh wound in his thigh. "One of the officers came along, and, looking at me, said, 'What's the matter with, you, boy?' 'Nothing,' I answered. 'Poor fellow,' exclaimed he, 'you are bleeding to death.' I looked down; the blood was gushing out of me. The day was very warm. Lee did well; but Washington wasn't very well pleased with him." General Lee he describes as "a large man. He had a most enormous nose. One day a man met him and turned his nose away. 'What do you do that for, you d–d rascal?' exclaimed he. 'I was afraid our noses would meet,' was his reply. He had a very large nose himself. Lee laughed and gave him a dollar."

Of Burgoyne's surrender he says, "The British soldiers looked down-hearted. When the order came to 'ground arms,' one of them exclaimed, with an oath, 'You are not going to have my gun!' and threw it violently on the ground, and smashed it. Arnold was a smart man; they didn't sarve him quite straight."[28]

He was at the encampment at Valley Forge. "Lady Washington visited the army. She used thorns instead of pins on her clothes. The poor soldiers had bloody feet." At Yorktown he shook hands with Cornwallis. He describes him as "a fine looking man; very mild. The day after the surrender, the Life Guard came up. Cornwallis sat on an old bench. 'Halt!' he ordered; then looked at us—viewed us."

Of the Indian warfare in the Mohawk valley, Mr. Milliner has broken recollections. Of the attack on Fort Stanwix, he gives the following graphic description: "The Indians burnt all before them. Our women came down in their shirt tails. The Indians got one of our young ones, stuck pine-splinters into it, and set them on fire. They came down a good body of 'em. We had a smart engagement

28. It is unlikely that seven-year-old Milliner witnessed the British surrender at Saratoga in October 1777; even if he accompanied his father's regiment at the time, the 1st New York was not at Saratoga. Milliner's statement that "they didn't sarve him quite straight" probably refers to the roles given to Benedict Arnold in the Continental army rather than to his treason.

with 'em, and whipped 'em. One of 'em got up into a tree—a sharp-shooter. He killed our men when they went after water. The colonel see where he was, and says, 'Draw up the twenty-four-pounder and load it with grape, canister, and ball.'[29] They did it. The Indians sat up in a crotch of the tree. They fired and shot the top of the tree off. The Indians gave a leap and a yell, and came down. Three brigades got there just in the nick of time. The Massachusetts Grenadiers and the Connecticut troops went forward, and the Indians fled."

In all, Mr. Milliner served six years and a half in the army. The following is a copy of his pension certificate:

> United States of America—War Department
> *Pension Claims.*
> This is to certify that Alexander Maroney, late a drummer in the Army of the Revolution, is inscribed on the Pension List Roll of the New York Agency, at the rate of eight dollars per month; to commence on the 19th day of September, 1819.
> *In witness whereof,* I have hereunto set my hand and affixed the seal of the War Department.
> John C. Calhoun.

Besides his service in the army, Mr. Milliner has served his country five years and a half in the navy. Three years of this service was on board the old frigate Constitution, he being in the action of February 20, 1814, in which she engaged the two British ships, the Cyane and the Levant, capturing them both. While following the sea he was captured by the French and carried into Guadaloupe. As prisoner there, he suffered hard treatment. Of the bread which he says he has eaten in seven kingdoms, he pronounces that in the French prison decidedly the worst.[30]

He still has the little tin case in which, in the old days of British seizure and search, he used to carry his protection papers.[31] The papers themselves are lost.

29. Twenty-four pounder, that is, a cannon capable of firing a 24-pound iron ball.

30. As discussed above, no documentary evidence of sea service by Alexander Milliner (or Maroney) has been found.

31. Protection papers, that is, papers proving that a man was not a deserted British seaman. Prior to the War of 1812, British ships stopped and searched American vessels in an effort to reclaim sailors who had absconded.

At the age of thirty-nine, Mr. Milliner married Abagail Barton, aged eighteen; and settled in Cortlandt county, New York. To my inquiry, how he came to settle there, his reply was, "O, I kind o' wandered round." For sixty-two years he and his wife lived together, without a death in the family or a coffin in the house. His wife died two years ago. They had had nine children, seven of whom are now living. The oldest was born in 1800. He has also forty-three grand children, seventeen great-grand-children, and three great-great-grand-children. At the time of his wife's death, Mr. Milliner was still able to cultivate his garden; his age being one hundred and two years.

Mr. Milliner's occupation since he settled down in life has been that of farming. His temperament has ever been free, happy, jovial, careless; and to this, doubtless, is largely owing the extreme prolongation of his life. He has been throughout life full of jokes; in the army he was the life of the camp; could dance and sing, and has always taken the world easily, "nothing troubling him over five minutes at a time," care finding it impossible to fasten itself upon him, and so, after trial, letting him alone. His spirits have always been buoyant, nothing depressing him.

Mention has been made of his wound at the battle of Monmouth. At another time a bullet passed through the head of his drum. At the time his photograph was taken he could still handle his drum, playing for the artist, with excellent time and flourishes which showed him to have been a master of the art. He sang also, in a clear voice, several songs, both amorous and warlike; singing half a dozen verses successively, giving correctly both the words and the tune.

His sight is as good yet as when young. He reads his Bible every day without the aid of glasses. His memory is clear respecting events which occurred eighty or ninety years ago; though he finds difficulty in giving long, connected accounts.

In size, he is small, more so than his picture would indicate. Though never robust, his health has always been good. This has not been from any special carefulness in his habits—in which he has been careless—rather giving himself and his health no thought. He uses tea and coffee, and still takes regularly his dram. His home is at present with his son, Hon. I. P. Milliner, of Adam's Basin. His every wish is gratified, so far as is compatible with his welfare; and

Alexander Milliner, photographed by Messrs. N. A. and R. A. Moore, 1864. (*Society of the Cincinnati*)

even when this is forbidden, still there is no necessity of denying him, since his wish, when expressed and nominally assented to, is at once forgotten by him; and if he is not reminded of it, is never thought of again.

In the present conflict with treason, Mr. Milliner's sympathies, as with all his surviving Revolutionary comrades, are enlisted most strongly on the side of the Union; he declaring that it is "too bad that this country, so hardly got, should be destroyed by its own people." He inquires every day or two about the army; and express-es the desire to live to see the rebellion crushed. At the outbreak of it, he wanted to take his drum and go down to Rochester, and beat for volunteers. Two years ago, in September, he presided over a meeting for raising recruits for the One Hundred and Fortieth New York Regiment. His presence at the meeting, it is said, caused great excitement and enthusiasm.

Upon his last birthday (his one hundred and fourth), the Pioneers of Monroe county—a veteran association whose head-quarters are at Rochester—went out in a body to Adam's Basin, to pay their respects to their aged associate. Arrived at the Basin, and marching in procession to the house where the old man resides, he appeared upon the steps, and was greeted with cheers. After many had shaken hands with him, the procession was re-formed, the old man heading it, and marched to the church, where, after the singing of Washington's Funeral Hymn by the Pioneers and a short historical address, Mr. Milliner stood up on a seat where all could see him, and thanking them for their kind attention, appealed to them all to be true to their country, saying that he had seen "worse looking visages than his own hung up by the neck." Since that time, his health has rapidly failed; and it is now unlikely that he will live to see another birthday.

5

William Hutchings

Massachusetts Militia

THINKING OF REVOLUTIONARY WAR VETERANS INVARIABLY conjures images of fighting at Bunker Hill, Trenton, Monmouth, or Yorktown, of freezing in winter at Valley Forge or Morristown, of trapping Burgoyne at Saratoga, or of leaving the farm fields around Lexington to heed Paul Revere's call to arms. But this wasn't the war experienced by thousands of soldiers who served short stints close to hometowns that saw no fighting. Muster rolls are filled with names of men who, according to their pension depositions, "saw no battle." It would be wrong, however, to perceive them as men who did no duty, suffered no hardship, bore no burden of their fledgling nation's defense. Great Britain had a highly mobile army supported by a powerful navy; British armed forces could strike anywhere on the American coast with little warning. This meant that every coastal town was under some level of threat during the entire war. This threat was heightened by American use of many small ports as havens for privateers, privately owned armed vessels that roamed the seas (with the permission of colonial governments called letters of marque) hoping to capture British-owned vessels laden with valuable goods.[1] The war made every American port a potential military base which therefore required defense. Most of that defense was provided by vigilant militiamen who awaited attacks that never came.

Among those who turned out to defend the local coast was sixteen-year-old William Hutchings. He spent his life in Maine, a region that was at the time part of the colony of Massachusetts. Born in York on October 6, 1764, he moved north in 1768 with his family to Penobscot, where his father established a farm. In 1779 a British post was established at Castine in Penobscot Bay that became the focus of an American attempt to dislodge it; after the American attack failed the Hutchings family moved to Newcastle,

1. Robert Gardiner, ed., *Navies and the American Revolution 1775–1783* (Annapolis, MD: Naval Institute Press, 1996), 66–69.

some distance south along the coast, for the remainder of the war. It was in Newcastle that Hutchings came of military age. In late May or early June 1781 he enlisted in a regiment of Massachusetts militia commanded by Colonel Samuel McCobb, an experienced officer who may have inspired zeal in a teenager anxious to serve his colony.[2] When Hutchings applied for a pension in 1832, his father deposed on his behalf that "he the said William Hutchings being then a Minor did by my consent inlist,"[3] and Rev. Hillard's 1864 biography also asserted that Hutchings had "enlisted at the age of fifteen." This is at odds with his service record that clearly has him serving at least from June 20, 1781 (when he was sixteen),[4] and even a statement from 1855 in his pension file says that he served June 26 to December 1, 1781, "5 mos. 10 days as private."[5]

The regiment, or at least Hutching's portion of it, marched to the coast and took post at a place called Cox's Head, an eminence that overlooks a channel among islands where the Kennebec River empties into the Atlantic Ocean. We have no details on what this "Troop of Volunteers" did during those months; not a single account is known to exist that describes their activities. There was surely much routine military duty including training; guards; procurement of provisions, fuel, and other supplies; maintaining and improving fortifications; and countless other tasks that filled the time but not in a memorable way. There may have been occasional alarms when hostile vessels were known to be in nearby waters or enemy incursions were expected. The soldiers probably spoke with excitement of far-off events like the movement of French troops from Rhode Island to threaten New York in July and

2. Samuel McCobb had been captain of a militia company at the beginning of the war and commanded companies in state and Continental regiments before becoming a colonel in the Massachusetts militia. Heitman, *Historical Register of Officers*, 366.

3. Pension file of William Hutchings, S. 22,320, Revolutionary War Pensions.

4. *Massachusetts Soldiers and Sailors of the American Revolution* (Boston: Wright & Potter Printing Co, 1901), 8:578, 8:591. This book includes an entry indicating that Hutchings received a "musket, etc." at "Camp Coxes Head" on June 8, 1781; but a subsequent entry for William "Hutshon" says that he was "engaged June 20, 1781." The two entries are cross-referenced to each other, and other details make it clear that they refer to the same man. Hutchings's pension file mentions that his name appears at "Hutshon" on some records.

5. Pension file of William Hutchings, S. 22,320, Revolutionary War Pensions.

August, and the British raid on Groton and New London, Connecticut, in September. Surely they celebrated when they heard news of the British surrender at Yorktown in October.[6] Although the young Hutchings was probably quite busy during his army career, in terms of the war it was uneventful. He was discharged on December 1, 1781, and although he was still young he never again entered military service.

Reading Hutchings's pension deposition, and Rev. Hillard's biography of him, gives the impression that he had no exposure to actual fighting during the American Revolution. He was, however, in the thick of Maine's fiercest battle in any war, and witness to one of the worst naval defeats in American history. It all occurred while his family lived in Penobscot two years before he joined the army.

In 1779 the British were looking for a new way to establish a presence in New England. They sent an expedition under Brigadier General Francis McLean[7] to Penobscot Bay with about seven hundred troops and a contingent of artificers. They landed without opposition and proceeded to build a fort on a peninsula projecting into the bay where the present-day town of Castine is situated.[8] Most of the warships that accompanied the expedition then sailed off to other stations, leaving three armed sloops and a number of transport ships to augment the land force.[9] Young but able-bodied, William Hutchings was among the local inhabitants called to assist in construction of the new post named Fort George. He joined in the work, but apparently soon left to go about his business because of his age. He was free to come and go as he pleased and made

6. News of the surrender on October 17 was first published in New England newspapers on October 27; it probably reached coastal Maine within a few days. *Providence Gazette, Boston Evening Post,* and *New Hampshire Gazette,* all issues of October 27, 1781.

7. Francis McLean was the Colonel of the 82nd Regiment of Foot and a brigadier general in the British army in America. Franklin B. Wickwire, "McLean, Francis," in *Dictionary of Canadian Biography,* vol. 4, University of Toronto/Université Laval, 2003–,biographi.ca/en/bio/mclean_francis_4E.html, accessed December 29, 2013.

8. Remains of British earthworks remain today in Fort George State Park, Castine, Maine.

9. For a detailed account of the Penobscot battle, see George E. Buker, *The Penobscot Expedition: Commodore Saltonstall and the Massachusetts Conspiracy of 1779* (Annapolis, MD: Naval Institute Press, 2002).

Photograph of William Hutchings by A. H. Dresser of Bucksport, Maine, October 6, 1865. (*Allan Janus collection*)

good use of this latitude. He went on board British warships, sold milk, and met sailors and officers.

A month after the British arrived an American expedition out of Boston came to unseat them. The Americans had assembled over forty ships and one thousand militia troops, a force that appeared ample to defeat the small British garrison in its unfinished works. General McLean, in spite of the poor odds, opted to defend his post. There ensued a three-week siege during which all sorts of spirited actions occurred: exchanges of gunfire between ships, bombardment of ships by shore batteries on both sides, sorties against fortified positions, scouting and skirmishing and sniping. Throughout all of it, young William Hutchings retained his freedom to pass from one side of the fight to the other. The siege ended badly for the Americans; they were unable to organize an effective assault on the incomplete but well-defended British works, and when a few additional British warships arrived the commanders of American vessels panicked and fled up the river where they scuttled their ships or ran them aground and burned them. The scattered seamen and soldiers made their way on foot back to Boston, suffering much on the way due to lack of provisions.[10]

Considering the wartime experience of William Hutchings, Rev. Hillard's account of him is strangely sparse. Hillard makes note of Hutchings having witnessed the siege of Penobscot but gives it barely a passing mention, as if it were of no particular importance. In reality, this was the most exciting time of his life, and he did talk about it extensively—but not, apparently, with Rev. Hillard. Two other Maine residents of the same era recorded reminiscences that Hutchings shared with them; physician Joseph L. Stevens, Jr., interviewed Hutchings in 1855 as did lawyer Joseph Williamson in 1860. In these two tellings, Hutchings related many personal anecdotes of his experiences during the siege, and his memory was keen: his recollection correlates well with first-hand accounts by other participants written when the events occurred. The interviews have been published before but have gone largely unnoticed, at least in terms of their connection with the old pensioner pic-

10. The aftermath is discussed in Buker, *The Penobscot Expedition.*

tured in Rev. Hillard's book. Hutchings's two narratives were not given as chronological stories of the siege, but instead as a series of separate episodes in the order that he happened to recall them. Below is the full text of these two interviews with no sentences altered, but merged and arranged sentence by sentence into a reasonably smooth narrative. It begins with some background on the location where the British fort was built and includes some of Hutchings's recollections unrelated to the events of 1779.

William Hutchings's Narrative of the Siege of Penobscot, and Other Reminiscences[11]

A good many years ago, I used to know a man named Conolly, who told me that he once found near the second Narrows, on or near the shore, a kind of chest pretty much covered over with moss or grass, as if it had been exposed to the weather many years. On opening it he found French goods, such as handkerchiefs, etc. As long ago as I can remember there was what was called the "Old French Fort,"[12] down by the shore below Banks's house.[13] There were a great many spruce poles around it and posts in the shore, when I was a boy. There used to be a considerable growth of oak there. I do not remember ever hearing that there were in old times any Mills about here belonging to Frenchmen—what used to be called the "Winslow" farm, at the head of Northern Bay, was a great while ago called "Frenchman's" farm, and the pond at the head of a stream that runs through it, was called "Frenchman's" pond, when I was a boy, and there was an old cellar there they used to call the old Frenchman's cellar. It may be all gone now. If not, you will find it between Perkins' store and the shore.

11. George A. Wheeler, *History of Castine, Penobscot and Brooksville, Maine* (Bangor, ME: Burr and Robinson, 1875), 322–328.

12. Fort Pentagöet, built early in the seventeenth century. "Fort Pentagouet," *Collections of the Maine Historical Society* 4 (1893), 113–123.

13. Aaron Banks, Jr.; the house, and many other landmarks described by Hutchings, can be seen on "The Chart of Penobscot," *Atlas of the American Revolution* (New York: Rand McNally, 1974), 156–157.

Doctor Calf (Calef) built the old Mann house about a year before the British came.[14] He was a Tory refugee. When the British came in I was at Fox Islands, with my uncle—where we went fishing in an open boat.[15] We had news of their coming, and when the fleet came in sight, uncle said, "there comes the devils." We started for home, and when the fleet followed us up we knew it was them. We reached Castine when they were firing guns for pilots.[16] Nine of the vessels came in. They anchored off Dice's Head, I should think by eleven o'clock. Their boats came ashore down at the beach, below Johnson's corner. I was there when they landed. As many as twenty officers came ashore. They all looked around as if they were considerably frightened. They didn't do much that day. I went home that night. Can't say if troops came next day or day after. When I went down they were camped in tents on the ridge to northeast of where the fort is.[17]

The British landed in front of Joseph L. Perkins' house, June 17, 1779, which stood on what is now the south eastern corner of Main and Water Streets. They seemed as frightened as a flock of sheep, and kept looking around them as if they expected to be fired on by an enemy hid behind the trees. This day they did not stop, but returned to their vessels. The next day they came on shore, and encamped on the open land east of where the fort now stands. They immediately began to fortify the place. In a short time the American expedition came, and orders were sent out for the inhabitants to come in and work. I helped to haul the first log into the south bastion. It was on the Sunday before the Americans arrived, and was the only Sunday on which I had to work in my life.[18] The peninsula was then covered with a heavy growth of trees. When

14. John Calef was a prominent loyalist resident of Penobscot; he kept a journal of the 1779 siege. John Calef, *The Siege of Penobscot by the Rebels* (London: G. Kearsleep, 1781). By "the old Mann house," Hutchings apparently refers to a subsequent owner of Calef's house.

15. This cluster of islands is in Penobscot Bay; today they are called North Haven and Vinalhaven after the two towns they contain.

16. Firing guns for pilots, that is, firing guns as signals for local harbor pilots to come out to the ships and help them steer into the unfamiliar waters.

17. These street names are still current in Castine, Maine.

18. Inhabitants were first called to work on July 19, so Hutchings probably refers to July 25, 1779. Calef, *The Siege of Penobscot*, entry for July 19, 1779.

the fort was built it was mostly spruce, and the trees were rather small, but farther to the westward there was a good deal of maple, beech, birch, etc.

General McLean was an excellent officer. He was very angry because the Tories drove off so many of the Americans by saying that the English were going to hang them. The old General didn't go about much, but the other officers used to. They went to Orland, to see Old Vyles' daughters.[19]

The frigate *Blonde* was one of the convoy that came with McLean.[20] She did not come in, but lay outside of the harbor. I used to go on board, to sell milk, &c. She was a beautiful ship—was not here at the time of the siege, had gone away.

There were three frigates—the *Albany*, *North* and *Nautilus*. The *Albany* carried sixteen guns, the *Nautilus* twenty-two, and the *North* twenty-eight.[21] She was an old French ship, and was not good for much of anything. Her guns were light-mounted. The *Albany* was commanded by an American. Mowatt was a Portland man.[22] I went aboard the *Nautilus*. I was a boy. One of my coun-

19. This is unlikely; although Joseph Viles did live in Orland, Maine, about ten miles northeast of the British fort, his daughters, born in 1765 and 1774, were too young to be the objects of advances by British officers. Henry Sweetser Burrage and Albert Roscoe Stubbs, *Genealogical and Family History of the State of Maine* (New York: Lewis Historical Publishing Co., 1909), 1:430.

20. HMS *Blonde* was a 32-gun frigate built by the French as *Le Blonde* and captured by the British in 1760. The ship escorted the initial British expedition to Penobscot and was among those that came to relieve the siege. The ship ran onto a rock and sank off of Cape Sable Island, Nova Scotia, on May 10, 1782; the rock is now called Blonde Rock. *Town and Country* magazine, vol. 14 (London: A. Hamilton, 1782), 502.

21. Hutchings overstates the size and armament of the British ships. All three were sloops, not frigates. There are discrepancies in various sources as to the number of guns each ship carried; one indicates that *Albany* carried 14, *Nautilus* carried 16, and *North* carried 18, all 6-pounders (that is, guns that fire solid balls weighing six pounds). Other sources indicate that *Albany* carried 16 and *North* as many as 24. Each ship also carried a number of half-pound swivel guns, which Hutchings may have included in his count. "List of the Navy, 1780–1783," Admiralty Library MSS 301/18, National Museum of the Royal Navy, Portsmouth; *Independent Chronicle and the Universal Advertiser* (Boston), July 8, 1779.

22. Hutchings was incorrect that one of the British ships was commanded by an American, or that Lieutenant Henry Mowat was from Portland. In 1775 Mowat led a squadron that attacked Portland, then called Falmouth; this may be the source of Hutchings's confusion.

trymen took me down below, and fed me pretty well, then told me he was a pressed man.[23] He had tried to run away, and got flogged for it. I saw two men flogged on the *Albany*. They can say what they please, when tied up, and one man told the officer he should run away again every chance.[24] An English soldier joined us on the Kennebec, and then ran into the country. He was brought back and court martialed, and sentenced to 200 lashes. The blood ran down and filled his shoes. When he had received 100, they had to take him down.[25]

General Lovell[26] built his works mostly of logs and brush. He had to cut away a great many trees to make a passage for his cannon balls to the fort. General McLean expected to be taken, and when his troops were driven back into the fort, the morning the American troops landed—July 28, 1779—he stood with the pennant halliards in his own hands all ready to strike the colors himself.[27] He said he had been in nineteen battles without getting beaten, but he expected he should be beaten in the twentieth one. The walls of the fort were so low at that time that I heard a soldier say he could jump over with a musket in each hand. McLean considered that every day the Americans delayed the attack was as good to him as another thousand men.

23. The British navy was allowed to press, or force, able-bodied seamen into service under certain circumstances. Here Hutchings refers to an American pressed to serve on a British warship, not an unusual circumstance. For a detailed study of this topic, see Denver Brunsman, *The Evil Necessity: British Naval Impressment in the Eighteenth-Century Atlantic World* (Charlottesville: University of Virginia Press, 2013).

24. In other words, a man was not held accountable for what he said while being flogged.

25. It is not clear how Hutchings could have known about this event as described; if he was in Kennebec, the event must have occurred after the siege, but then Hutchings would not have been in a position to know about court-martial and punishment unless he was told about it later.

26. Brigadier General Solomon Lovell of Massachusetts commanded the American militia on the expedition.

27. That is, McLean was ready to lower the fort's flag as a sign of surrender.

My father was among the patriots who joined the Americans. He was stationed part of the time at Hainey's point,[28] and always thought he killed an English soldier there. A party of English came to drive the Americans away, and most of them speedily retreated; but my father and a few others stopped to give them a parting shot, when the boat should come in good range. We thought they would come in above and cut us off. As soon as the boats went off, the guard ran off. My father came near shooting one of our men who had run off. He was in the bushes, and started up. Father saw him and brought his gun to fire on him. He had a fur cap on, and father saw a mark on the back of it. The guard at Hainey's Point all ran off but five, who fired and killed one man—the first who was killed. One of the guard afterward said to him at Mrs. Hainey's house that when my father fired he saw a soldier in one of the boats fall, and heard him cry out. My father is said to have done it on the second shot, and the Tories (the commanding officer didn't say it) said he would be hung. Mrs. Hainey was along and she subsequently reported this at head quarters, and we supposed it the reason of our family being driven away. Mrs. Hainey told of it, and my mother was so frightened we had to move away. Ah! hard and trying times those were!

I worked on the battery at Wescott's in all, eight days. In Wescott's battery there were three guns, one 12-lb., one 6-lb., and one 3-lb. brass field piece,[29] which was lost overboard off Stover Perkins' point, when the Americans were trying to carry it off. It lays there now, I suppose—a little way from the shore. The transport must have come as nigh as she could. It probably slipped out of the slings.

We kept up a hot fire on the ships, and drove the men ashore and below. We could hear our shots go—thud—into them. We shot an anchor from Wescott's battery off the *Santillana*[30] near Hatch's

28. Haney's Point, or Haney's Plantation, was across the river to the east. This skirmish appears to have occurred on August 7, the only time that British sources mention landing troops there, but none report any men killed. There had been numerous casualties prior to that day, and it is possible that Hutchings conflated separate events. Calef, *The Siege of Penobscot*, entry for August 7, 1779.

29. The cannons are referred to by the weight of the iron balls that they fired.

30. The *St. Helena* or *Santilena*, a privateer ship that had been captured and put into service by the British.

Point. Three or four ships lay along there. We cut away an anchor hanging at the bows of one of them. I saw it at low tide, and suppose I might have got it, if I had had spunk enough. I marked where it fell, as I thought sometime or other I might want to get it up. The *Santillana* was a very nice ship. The *St. Helena* [*Santillana*] was a letter-of-marque, of fourteen guns. She was not in the regular service. The old *Providence*[31] was an old vessel. She fell over and stove her broadside in. She was one of the British fleet. They hauled the transports ashore, when the Americans came. Otter Rock was named for the ship *Otter*, which went on the rock close by, at the eastward of it, going out, I think.[32]

Nautilus Island was named after the *Nautilus*, and I suppose I saw the caper that was the occasion of it. It was reported that there was to be a combined attack on the fort and frigates, at a set time, by the Americans. I went with a number of others to the high land in Brooksville, opposite Negro Island, but it did not take place. At that, or another time, I recollect seeing some of the American fleet drop in behind Nautilus Island and fire across the bar at the English ships. The *Hazard*[33] and other vessels, ran in behind the island, and fired across the bar, and raked the ships that lay across the mouth of the harbor. They cut or slipped their cables, and dropped up further. Their last shot ploughed up the dry sod near Hatch's house, and set considerable of it on fire. Nautilus Island used to be called Banks's Island; was called Nautilus Island after that.[34]

One night the Americans undertook to surprise the English but they fell in with the British guard at Banks's battery, and had a sharp fight. Quite a number were killed on both sides. I afterwards saw, up by the narrows, some bloody uniforms, tied up in a blanket, that had been stripped from the English soldiers killed that

31. There was an armed sloop in the American fleet named *Providence*; it is not clear what ship Hutchings refers to here when he describes an old British transport by this name.

32. There was no warship named *Otter* on the expedition. If Hutchings is correct about this name derivation, he may be referring to a transport vessel.

33. The *Hazard*, a 14-gun ship of the Massachusetts state navy.

34. This rock may have been named for, or by the crew of, the *Nautilus*, but given that British writers used the name during the siege it probably wasn't named for this specific event.

night. Major Sawyer was killed, or drowned, in a boat that was sunk by a cannon ball fired from the fort, while it was passing from the fleet to Nautilus Island.[35] A cannon shot from the battery on Nautilus Island came in the fort gate and passing between General McLean and one of his officers, killed an ox belonging to my father—which he had raised himself. Being so young I was allowed to go off and on the peninsula, but the soldiers sometimes used to call me "a damned little rebel." A drummer was killed, the night of the skirmish, at the battery near Banks's house, and, for a good many years after, people used to say that they could hear his ghost drumming there at midnight. I saw both Lovell and Wadsworth.[36] I did not like the appearance of Lovell very well, but Wadsworth was a beautiful man. There was no canal dug across the neck at that time.

When the siege was raised the guns were carried across to Matthew's point to be put on board the transports. In the hurry of getting them on board a brass four-pounder was lost overboard. I saw as many as 50 or 60 cannon the English got from the fleet up the river. They all lay at high water mark on the shore, loaded, and were fired off, to see if they were cracked, or anything the matter with them. The old wreck on the shore down below Hatch's was the *Providence*. The *Providence* was an old transport, that troops come over in. She fell over there, I believe, and stove her side in. About that ship *Providence*, you needn't be afeared to assert it as truth, because I know all about it. Hatch's barn was used as a hospital. I was there after the siege was raised, and the floor was then covered with beds so thick that there was scarcely room to pass between them. The poor fellows groaned a good deal when the doctors dressed their wounds. I believe most of those who died there were buried on the lower side of the road.

finis

35. Major Samuel Sawyer was killed during the fight for Banks's battery on August 1, 1779. Solomon Lovell, *The Original Journal of General Solomon Lovell, Kept during the Penobscot Expedition, 1779* (Weymouth, MA: Weymouth Historical Society, 1881), entry for August 1, 1779.
36. Brigadier General Peleg Wadsworth of the Massachusetts Militia.

With the siege lifted and peninsula firmly in British hands, the Hutchings family fled the area. William's father had taken up arms with the attackers and decided to abandon his farm rather than face retribution from Tories. They relocated only a few dozen miles away in New Castle, where William joined the militia in 1781.

In 1782, his militia service over, William Hutchings left his family in New Castle and returned to Penobscot. He found the family farm burned, the fences gone. The British post had become a base for loyalist privateers that preyed on shipping from ports north of Boston. Most prominent of those vessels was the brig *Miriam* commanded by Richard Pomroy, which had taken a number of American merchantmen and in August 1782 clashed with American militia at Cape Porpoise.[37] In September, the *Miriam* was at anchor in Penobscot when the small Massachusetts Navy sloop *Winthrop* commanded by Captain George Little boldly approached in the evening.[38] Pretending to be a captured vessel, they deceived sentries on the *Miriam* into letting the *Winthrop* come alongside. Crewmen from the *Winthrop* seized the *Miriam* and both ships headed out of the harbor while being fired on from shore. Loss of his ship was a great embarrassment to Pomroy; Hutchings related the story to Joseph L. Stevens:

> I remember when Pomroy was cut out by Little. He chased Pomroy about, but couldn't bring him to an engagement.[39] Little said he would have him, if he followed him to hell. Pomroy had taken a coasting vessel which Little retook. Little got a whale-boat at Fox Islands, which he left with some men, below Nautilus Island, to make his escape in, if necessary. Pomroy had a 14-gun Brig; Little had a 12-gun Sloop. He came in on top of the tide, just at the close of day—before dark. When the sentry hailed him, he replied that he was a prize from Fox Island. "Who commands her?" "Peter Littlejohn."[40] He ran alongside of the brig, and told them to heave him a warp, as he had lost both anchors in Fox

37. *New England Chronicle* (Boston), October 3, 1782.
38. *Providence Gazette*, September 28, 1782.
39. That is, Little had been chasing Pomroy's ship during the previous days.
40. Little used the name of the commander of a sloop that Pomroy had recently captured. *New England Chronicle* (Boston), October 3, 1782.

Island thoroughfare. He had his men all ready, and jumped aboard with them, and took her. The sloop kept right on, and stood out of the harbor, but the brig had to make a couple of tacks. The people collected to look on, and Captain Little afterwards said he might have swept the streets as he went by. He was fired on from the fort, and the men ran down to the old French fort and fired. Commissary McLaughlin told a man (I heard him), that he delivered out 1700 rounds. It was said that Little picked up bullets by the bucketful from his deck, where they fell, after striking among the sails and rigging. A shot from the sloop, or brig, when going out of the harbor, struck a crowbar, and drove it through a hogshead of rum that stood in the King's store, about ten rods below the Fort gate. William Redhead told me that shot cost him one hogshead of rum. He was a sort of deputy Commissary, and came over with the British. He married old Banks' daughter.[41] Pomroy was a Tory. He and most of his crew were ashore. Next day the British officers laughed at him. They thought very much of Little.

When Little came, I had come back from the Kennebec, (a year before father) and worked here with the neighbors. I was then at old Mr. Samuel Wescott's. I had gone up to bed, and was leaning on a chest by the window. I heard a great firing of guns, and couldn't think what it all meant. Wescott was on the peninsula, and when he came home he told us all about it. I went down the next day and saw Pomroy, who looked as if he had been stealing sheep, and had lost all the friends he had in the world.

When the war ended, the Hutchings family returned to their land, rebuilt the farm and thrived in Penobscot. Hutchings's father lived until 1834, only two years after giving a deposition in support of his son's pension application.[42] William Hutchings farmed, cut lumber, and for a time was master of a coastal vessel. Because of this latter occupation, according to one account, he "ever after bore

41. William Reidhead, a British commissary worker who settled in Penobscot after the war, kept a journal during the 1779 siege of Penobscot. He married Olive Banks, daughter of Aaron Banks of Penobscot. See "William Reidhead's Journal, 1779," *Maine Historical Magazine* 5 (1890), 226–231.

42. This deposition survives in the pension file of William Hutchings, S. 22320, Revolutionary War Pensions.

the title of Captain Hutchings." At around thirty years of age he adopted the Methodist religion; later it was said that he "for many years, has advocated and practiced total abstinence from all intoxicating drinks." Until his last days he impressed people with his memory, so keen that he could relate "an incident occurring in Castine harbor when he was about four years old." He even recalled his own discourses with other veterans: "An interesting circumstance was related by him of having once conversed with a British soldier, afterwards settled at Brooksville, who was in the assault on Bunker Hill. After the first fire of the Americans, looking around, he saw standing only four besides himself, of those who had marched up to the redoubt."[43]

With the publication of the list of last pensioners in 1864, William Hutchings became nationally known; his survival to see the end of the Civil War increased his celebrity. The Fourth of July celebrations in 1865 were extra special to a nation that had finally achieved peace after its most bitter struggle. In Maine, plans were made for Hutchings to be a central part of the commemoration. The person who arranged the visit wrote a letter describing his first meeting with Hutchings, which appeared in the newspaper on the day of the celebrations:

> I found him in excellent health and full of spirit. After I told him about the preparations that are being made for him, and about the salutes that were to be fired at Fort Knox and at Bangor, he took me by the hand and, with tears in his eyes, he said, "It is too great an honor to bestow on me. Blessed be God," he exclaimed, "I feel that I gain strength every day, and that He will support me. I have great faith in God, that He will give me strength to go there and return again."
>
> He is wide awake, and will surprise you all by his strength and ability.... Mr. Hutchings told me today that the first time he was ever in Bangor was in May 1784. At that time there were but three houses in the place—one a log-house on the west side of the stream, and two frame-houses on the east side.... He said that he thought to himself at the time that it was a very lonesome

43. The quotations here are from William Hutchings's obituary, *Bangor Daily Whig & Courier*, May 16, 1866.

place, and that if he ever came there again it would be because he was brought by the eagles.[44]

A revenue cutter transported Hutchings up the Penobscot River to Bangor; along the way the guns of Fort Knox, guarding a narrow point in the river, fired a salute to welcome the old veteran. The Bangor newspaper advertised his expected presence at the "Ceremonies of the Day," the biggest celebrations that Maine had ever seen.[45] With some 35,000 people in attendance, a great parade started the fete. William Hutchings rode in an open carriage escorted by an honor guard, leading a contingent of veterans of subsequent conflicts including many from the War of 1812. After the parade were ceremonies: a speech by the mayor, an invocation, band music, and then "the old patriot, Mr. Hutchings, said a few words while sitting upon the stage, but in so low a tone as to be inaudible to the audience." Fortunately the local newspaper captured his words in full:[46]

> At the age of fifteen I enlisted for the defence of my country–and I have stood by her in all her subsequent periods. I have always been in favor of my country. I was through the battle of Bagaduce.[47] Our shipping on the Penobscot was all destroyed, and our soldiers were obliged to fly through the woods to the Kennebec. My father was obliged to flee with the rest. When he returned the tories threatened his life. Mother was so distressed that she coaxed father to move away. He got up a party and went to Damariscotta,[48] where we lived till the war was over. I was there all the time except when I was in the service of my country. When peace was declared we returned to Bagaduce. Our buildings were burned, fences all gone, father poor and mother sick. There were ten children to be supported by father's

44. *Bangor Daily Whig & Courier,* July 4, 1865.
45. *Bangor Daily Whig & Courier,* July 4, 1865. A revenue cutter was a government ship used to inspect cargoes of merchant vessels to insure that cargoes were legitimate and import duties were paid.
46. *Bangor Daily Whig & Courier,* July 6, 1865.
47. Hutchings uses the name of the Bagaduce River to describe the region where it empties into Penobscot Bay.
48. Newcastle and Damariscotta are on opposite sides of the Damariscotta River; Damariscotta was not incorporated as a separate town until 1848.

labor and mine, for I was then in my 18th year. It was a gloomy time, but God prospered us.

I don't know what will be done with the men that made this cursed, wicked rebellion. Jeff. Davis and the assassins of our noble President ought to be treated as God's law says: "Whoso sheddeth man's blood, by man shall his blood be shed."

Such a wicked thing as Jeff. Davis[49] attempted was never done before nor never will be done again by man. The papers say he don't like pea soup. I guess the poor, dear boys that he starved to death would have been glad to have got pea soup or bean broth. He ought to go hungry. I have no sympathy with Copperheads[50] who support Jeff. Davis. I call them chowder heads. The true meaning of a Copperhead, is a man without principle of any kind.

I have been much troubled lately because it seems as though they wasn't going to allow all the loyal men to vote. The black man is made free, and I can't comprehend how a freeman can be deprived of the liberty of the ballot box. God's family is a free family. Christ made all men free, and no human being can help it. The negroes must not be deprived of their rights. The President will not permit it–Congress will not permit it–and if they will, God will not permit it–never!–never!!–never!!!–NEVER!!!!

My heart is filled with joy that this rebellion is put down. And, dear soldiers, it does my heart good to know that you have returned home. I have always prayed for you, and the blessed God has answered my prayers. The country owes you a debt that they can never pay. You have put down this wicked, awful rebellion, and the good God will reward you. I have lost grand-sons in this war, but it is a glorious privilege to die for one's country. Thank God, there are no tories in my family.

I thank you all for the great honor you have done me; it is almost too great for me to bear. I do not deserve it. They told me it would kill me, but I could never die any better than celebrating the Fourth of July. Good bye–God bless you all.

49. Jefferson Davis, president of the Confederacy during the American Civil War.

50. Copperheads were northerners who opposed the Civil War, preferring to make peace with the separatist states.

Hutchings was conveyed to his carriage and taken away to the strains of a march while people watched, hat in hand, offering him greetings and praise as he passed. The old soldier returned to his home the next day "apparently very little fatigued by the journey hither, and the part he took in the procession," and his family published a notice of thanks to those in Bangor who had put such effort into honoring and caring for their patriarch.[51] The speech was carried in newspapers around the nation. At some point during his visit to Bangor, Hutchings was photographed wearing the "elegant dressing gown" that had been presented to him days earlier; copies of the photograph could be purchased in town.[52] He was photographed again on October 6 by A. H. Dresser of Bucksport, Maine, wearing the same suit that he had worn for Nelson Augustus Moore in 1864.

William Hutchings lived for another ten months; he died at his home on May 3, 1866, having lived for one hundred and one years, six months and twenty-six days. According to his obituary, "The health of Mr. Hutchings had been for several weeks declining; and after suffering much, on Sunday, April 29, the signs of approaching death were manifest. But as his life had been unusually protracted, so he was long in dying. It was not until the noon of Thursday that he entered into rest. He retained his consciousness to the last; patient, calmly, confidently trusting in that Saviour whom, for 68 years, as a professed disciple, he had endeavored to follow." He was laid to rest at the family farm five days later, the funeral attended by a large number of relations spanning five generations. In accordance with his own wishes, the funeral sermon was from Matthew 22:40, "On these two commandments hang all the law and the prophets." One of his daughters read a poem composed for the occasion, to the words of which his last request was carried out: the flag covering his coffin was raised to fly over his grave.[53]

51. *Bangor Daily Whig & Courier*, July 6, 1865.

52. Advertisements for "Photographs of Wm. Hutchings, one of the four surviving heroes of the Revolutionary war, for sale at twenty five cents each, at Sawyer's Photograph Rooms, 2 1/2 Kendukeag Bridge" appeared on July 12 and continued into August in the *Bangor Daily Whig & Courier*. An engraving based on this picture appears in *Frank Leslie's Illustrated Newspaper*, May 26, 1866, incorrectly described as being "from a photograph by G. E. Collins, of Bucksport, Maine."

53. The sermon given at the funeral and the stanzas read over his grave are all included in his obituary. *Bangor Daily Whig & Courier*, May 16, 1866.

William Hutchings in the dressing gown presented to him at the Fourth of July celebrations in Bangor, 1865, photographed by S. W. Sawyer. (*Maine Historic Preservation Commission*)

By the time William Hutchings was old enough to join the militia in 1781, the war was winding down; the eight months or so that he spent with a Massachusetts militia company on the coast of Maine seem to have been uneventful. There is no evidence that he or other militiamen received any sort of uniform clothing. Like many American soldiers during the war, he probably served in the clothing he wore when he arrived for service.

The young soldier depicted here wears civilian clothing, including a skirted vest and single-breasted coat. The coat is similar in style to the one prescribed by the Massachusetts Provincial Congress for use by forces from the colony in 1775. Called a bounty coat because it was promised to each soldier upon enlistment (but not necessarily delivered in all cases), it was a simple brown woolen jacket with cast metal buttons very much like typical working man's clothing of the era. The militia man's black felt hat has a narrow brim that is not folded, or cocked. He wears a printed cotton handkerchief around his neck. He has straight-legged trousers and no gaiters or leggings to keep fouling out of his shoes. William Hutchings was issued a musket when he joined the militia; the weapon depicted here is a British land pattern musket, widely used on both sides of the conflict. The soldier carries a bayonet in a sling over one shoulder and a cartridge pouch slung over the other. As did any soldier upon extended military service from home, he wears a knapsack filled with spare clothing and necessities upon his back.

For more on uniforms of Massachusetts forces, see Henry M. Cook, "The Massachusetts Bounty Coat of 1775," *Brigade Dispatch* 28:3 (Autumn 1998), 2–10.

Drawing by Eric H. Schnitzer

The Pension Deposition of William Hutchings[54]

On this twenty sixth day of September, A.D. 1832, personally appeared in open Court, before the Hon. Job Nelson, Esquire, Judge of the Court of Probate within & for the County of Hancock aforesaid now sitting, William Hutchings a resident of Penobscot in the County of Hancock aforesaid aged sixty eight years, who being first duly sworn according to law, doth on his oath, make the following declaration in order to obtain the benefit of the act of congress passed June 7th 1832.

That he entered the service of the United States under the following named officers, & served as herein stated. In a Regiment of Massachusetts Militia commanded by Col. Samuel McCobb, (he does not recollect that there was any Lieut. Col. with the regiment) Major White[55] (George Ulmer[56] was Adjutant of the regiment) in the company commanded by Capt. Benjamin Lemmonds,[57] Lieut. Samuel Lemmonds,[58] Ensign, not recollected, that he entered the service at New Castle then in the Commonwealth of Massachusetts, now in the State of Maine where he then resided in the spring of the year 1780 or 1781, as a volunteer, for six months, & served a little more than six months, & was discharged about Christmas the same year, the day of the month he does not recollect. That he joined the regiment at a place called Cox's Head, at the mouth of Kennebec River, now in the state of Maine, where he was stationed during the whole time of his service, six months, & was there discharged after having served a little more than six months. That he was born in the year 1764, at York then in Massachusetts, now in the state of Maine. That he has no record of his age.

---

54. Pension deposition of William Hutchings, S. 22320, Revolutionary War Pensions.

55. Major John White of the Massachusetts militia.

56. The pension files include a George Ulmer from Lincoln County, Maine, where Hutchings and all of his officers served; this man's pension deposition mentions militia service only from 1777 to 1780, so it is not clear if the same man is named here.

57. Captain Benjamin Lemont of the Massachusetts militia.

58. Lieutenant Samuel Lemont, of the Massachusetts militia, Benjamin's younger brother.

That he has no written discharge.

That he now lives, and has lived ever since the Revolutionary War, in the town of Penobscot aforesaid.

That there were no continental troops[59] stationed near him during his service.

That Charles Hutchings & Jeremiah Jones whose depositions are hereto annexed, know of & can testify to his service as above stated.

That the Rev. William Mason & Pelatiah Leach Esquires are his neighbors, & can testify as to his character for veracity & their belief of his services as a soldier of the revolution.

He hereby relinquishes every claim whatever to a pension or annuity except the present, & declares that his name is not on the pension role of the agency of any state.

---

59. That is, there were only militia troops in the region where he served.

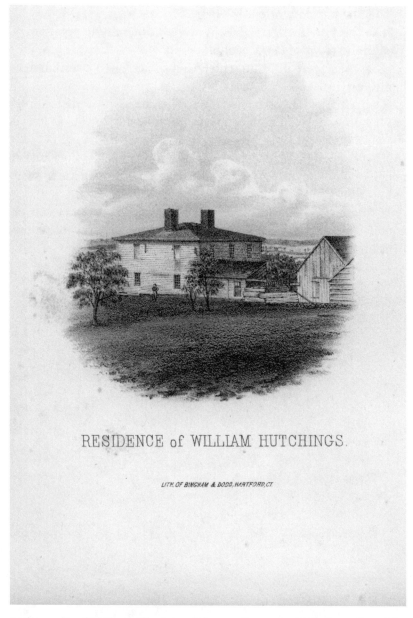

RESIDENCE of WILLIAM HUTCHINGS.

LITH. OF BINGHAM & DODD, HARTFORD, CT.

Lithograph of William Hutchings's home, Summer 1864, from *Last Men of the Revolution*. (*Society of the Cincinnati*)

William Hutchings

From E. B. Hillard, *The Last Men of the Revolution* (1864)

WILLIAM HUTCHINGS, WHOSE PHOTOGRAPH IS THE FIFTH IN the series, was born in York, York county, Maine, (then Massachusetts,) in 1764. He is, therefore, in his one hundred and first year.

Mr. Hutchings' connection with the war of the Revolution was but limited. He enlisted at the age of fifteen for the coast defense of his own state; and this was the only service in which he was engaged during the war. The only fighting which he saw was at the siege of Castine, where he was taken prisoner; but the British, declaring it a shame to hold as prisoner one so young, promptly released him.

His pension, until the late addition to it, was only twenty-one dollars and sixty-six cents.

The father of Mr. Hutchings had in his early manhood been familiar with military service, having served in the French War and been engaged in the siege and capture of Louisburg. In his old age he used to say that he had served under George II, George III, and also under George Washington, and was ready to serve under Madison. He lived to see his descendants of the fifth generation, by some of whom he was followed to the grave. At the time of his death, there were living, of those who derived their life through him, ten children, eighty-eight grand-children, two hundred and thirty-five great-grand-children, and seventeen great-great-grand-children,—in all, three hundred and fifty.

At the time of the capture of Louisburg he was a youth of only sixteen years of age, having been born in 1742. In 1768 he removed with his family from York to Penobscot—William, the subject of our sketch, being then four years old. The region at that time was mainly a wilderness, Mr. Hutchings, senior, being one of the earliest settlers in it. Here he remained for ten or twelve years, clearing a farm and establishing a home under the usual conditions of hardship and suffering incident to pioneer life. His son still recalls those experiences of childhood in his father's house. At times, he says, they were scarcely able to obtain food enough to satisfy the cravings of hunger; and he has dug clams for their meal, when he was obliged to stop and rest while at his work from faintness through want of food. They were finally, however, beginning to live comfortably when the British took possession of the neighboring town of Castine, and drove his father from his home, who fled with his family to Newcastle, where he abode till the close of the war, while William remained to fight the foe.

Shortly after the close of the war, Mr. Hutchings was married, at the age of twenty-two years. As the fruits of this union, there were born to him fifteen children, all but one of whom lived to be married. He has been throughout life an early riser and a hard worker; not particularly regular in his habits, often going without food till he could get what he relished; especially, living near the sea, and being fond of sea food, delaying his meal until it could be procured. He smokes regularly, and uses spirituous liquors moderately. His mind is still vigorous, though his body is feeble. Memory is good, retaining dates especially, so that he is a referee in the family in matters of history. He is deeply interested in the present conflict, his whole soul being enlisted in the cause of his country. Speaking of General Grant and his prospects of success in his campaign against Richmond, he concluded by saying, "Well, I know two old folks up here in Maine who are praying for him."[60]

He has lost four or five grand-children in the war.

His views on the subject of slavery are radical, he declaring that "God will never suffer it to exist in this country."

The old man now lives in the house which he himself built. It stands on an elevation at the head of Penobscot Bay, surrounded by the rugged headlands of the region, above which, seaward, in the distance, rise the blue peaks of Mount Desert; while in the hollow of the hills beneath quietly ebbs and flows the never-resting sea.

60. Referring to current events in the Civil War.

William Hutchings, photographed by Messrs. N. A. and R. A. Moore, 1864. (*Society of the Cincinnati*)

6

Adam Link

Pennsylvania Militia

THE FRENCH AND INDIAN WAR ENDED WHEN A TREATY WAS signed in Paris in February 1763. Great Britain's colonists in America relished the news not only because it brought peace to their land, but because it opened the way for unrestricted expansion westward into the lush and lucrative frontiers of the North American continent. No longer would Indian tribes inhabiting these lands have assistance from the French military. Settlement, a great economic engine, was poised for explosive growth.

The British government, however, did not share this view. They saw the importance of balancing their own settlers' needs with the native inhabitants' sovereignty; they had no interest in sustained hostilities between colonists and Indians, and saw the economic potential of fur trading and other harmonious pursuits. It was these interests that led to the Proclamation of 1763, announced in October, which put Indians in America under protection of the crown and established a strict western boundary on colonial settlement.[1] Under the proclamation, all land west of the Allegheny Mountains was Indian territory. Not only was settlement not allowed beyond the headwaters of rivers flowing to the east, but any settlers already west of the line extending along the Appalachian mountain range were required to abandon their lands and move east. It was even illegal to purchase land from the Indians, a prohibition necessitated by a series of fraudulent purchases previously made. The anticipated great westward expansion would not occur, at least not immediately and not without tight government control.

The proclamation made allies of natives who had struggled against the onslaught of European settlement. But it was wildly unpopular with colonists. For obvious reasons it alienated those

1. For a detailed discussion of the settlement policies and of the frontier war in general, see Jack M. Sosin, *The Revolutionary Frontier 1763–1783* (Albuquerque: University of New Mexico Press, 1967).

who were forced to abandon settlements west of the Allegheny border; it was also offensive to those near the border who despised the notion of being allied to the tribes with whom they had fought so recently. Closer to the coast, speculators with aspirations for land brokering or business ventures dependent on the frontier's natural resources were thwarted. The proclamation might bring peace, but at an economic cost many colonists were unwilling to accept. Subsequent treaties in 1768 and 1770 extended the boundary farther west, as far as the Ohio River on the western border of Pennsylvania, but tensions and hostilities continued unabated.

The British government had no illusions that laws alone would bring about peaceful coexistence in America. To enforce the treaty boundaries, construction began on a line of military posts. This spread resentment from the frontier settlers and land speculators to all walks of life in the colonies, for building and garrisoning these installations required funds to be raised by levying taxes on the colonists. The issue of taxation without representation loomed large, and the Proclamation of 1763 was instrumental in initiating those taxes. Although 1763 brought peace to America, the proclamation set the groundwork for another war a dozen years later. Often upstaged by subsequent events, the proclamation directly affected the lives of thousands of colonists in ways they perceived as negative and were unwilling to tolerate. Among those whose lives would be changed was a three-year-old boy named Adam Link.

The Proclamation of 1763, with its subsequent treaties and visible efforts by the British military to enforce them, not only contributed to the events that led to the American Revolution; it ensured that American Indian tribes would support the British government's efforts to suppress the rebellion. The frontier had been a turbulent place during the interwar years; the 1775 outbreak of hostilities along the coast caused frontier violence to escalate. The chaotic fighting in the western reaches of the colonies is widely overlooked in studies of the war's influential campaigns and battles, perhaps because the scale was smaller and the commanders less famous. But to the soldiers and families in this war zone the conflict was real, immediate, long, and bloody.

Adam Link was born in 1760 in the region of Pennsylvania near Fort Necessity that had figured in the onset of the French and Indian War.[2] In his pension depositions Link referred to the area as Washington County, but the region with that name was not defined until 1781; at the time of his birth it was part of Westmoreland County. While his family lived there the boundary between Pennsylvania and Virginia was disputed, making it impossible to know which colony the family considered themselves residents of. Maybe it didn't matter to them; their immediate concerns were survival and protecting their interests.[3]

By the time Link came of military age, war was in full swing in the western reaches of the colony near the Ohio River. It was a very savage, personal sort of warfare among opponents vying for the right to inhabit the land rather than over principles, laws, and governance. Exigencies of service took precedence over regulations and formalities; men often served when there was need, regardless of their legal obligations and without records of enlistment and discharge. This makes it quite difficult to determine the accuracy of Adam Link's statements in his pension depositions and the account by Rev. Hillard. The depositions of several other pensioners, although each with their own vagaries, at least allow Link's information to be framed in terms of what is plausible even though the absence of official contemporary documents like muster rolls makes it impossible to be certain of his service.

The Pennsylvania government passed its first law mandating militia service on March 17, 1777; prior to that the colony had had no established militia, relying instead on voluntary service and occasional temporary militia acts. The new militia system, however, mandated service for men from ages 18 to 53, meaning that Adam Link was still too young to be drafted.[4] He could serve as a

2. The various papers in Adam Link's pension folder give his year of birth sometimes as 1761, but most frequently as 1760. Pension file of Adam Link, S. 1771, Revolutionary War Pensions.

3. In his 1833 deposition Link claimed to have marched to Wheeling on the Ohio River after joining the militia in Washington County, but in his 1852 deposition he claimed that his family settled in Wheeling in 1775. The true location of their residence has not been determined. Pension file of Adam Link, S. 1771, Revolutionary War Pensions.

Adam Link's 1855 deposition in support of his claim for a pension. (*National Archives*)

substitute for someone else, but in his pension deposition he explicitly stated that he did not do so. He nonetheless claimed that on June 1, 1777, he joined the militia from his county and marched out under Captain David Williamson.[5] A reasonable explanation for this discrepancy is that he simply recalled the year incorrectly, and was drafted not in 1777 but in 1778 when he was 18 years old. He indicates that Captain Williamson was promoted to colonel during this first tour of duty, which seems to correspond to the summer of 1778.[6] But it is also entirely possible that Link recollected inaccurately the tour during which Williamson was promoted, and had turned out for militia service when he was underage because the need for soldiers was great. Being on the frontier in territory that had recently been disputed between Pennsylvania and Virginia, the Pennsylvania settlers may have been following the long-established Virginia militia law's age guidelines instead of their own newly enacted rules. A fellow soldier deposed that "there was but little system observed at that time in the militia regulations there,"[7] a simple statement that underscores the difficulty of documenting any individual's activities.

For simplicity, the remainder of this discussion will use the years given by Link even though it is possible that the actual timeline began a year later. The fledgling soldier claimed to have spent six months at an outpost called Dement's Fort,[8] one of many small posts that afforded protection against raids and provided a jumping-off point for scouting expeditions and counterstrikes. This is far in excess of the two-month term of service mandated by the militia law, which also was structured so that men would not be called out for back-to-back tours. But actual practice was based on neces-

4. Thomas Verenna, "Explaining Pennsylvania's Militia," *Journal of the American Revolution*, June 17, 2014, allthingsliberty.com/2014/06/explaining-pennsylvanias-militia/.

5. For more on Williamson's career and exploits, see R. Douglas Hurt, *The Ohio Frontier: Crucible of the Old Northwest, 1720–1830* (Bloomington: Indiana University Press, 1996).

6. The date of Williamson's promotion has not been found, but other pension depositions suggest that it occurred sometime in 1778.

7. Pension deposition of Isaac Ellis, W. 10013, Revolutionary War Pensions.

8. The location of this fort has not been determined; it is mentioned in only a few pension depositions. The Dement family were prominent settlers in the Wheeling area.

sity, not regulations, in places where settlers were protecting their homes. Similarly lengthy tours are described in the statements of other pensioners, some of whom expressed their service as several consecutive terms of one or two months each and others who referred to single tours of four, five, or six months. One of the most detailed claims was made by Isaac Ellis, who also served under Captain Williamson. Although recorded in 1833 when he was 80 years old, Ellis's description of his 1777 service provides precious details that may explain the discrepancies between Adam Link's deposition and the militia laws:

> That he [Ellis] entered the service of the United States under the following named officers and served as herein stated that is to say being a resident of the County of Washington in the western part of the state of Pennsylvania he did the early part of the month of June in the year 1777 enter the service of the United States as a draft militia man in the company of Capt David Williamson upon a tour of two months and was immediately thereupon appointed to orderly sergeant of his said company and served as such during the whole of his said tour. That immediately after his entry into the service as abovenamed he was detached with 30 or 40 other men composing a part of his afsd [aforesaid] company under the direction & command of Lieut. Eleazor Williamson who was lieut of the said company to Cross Creek about two miles from its place in Washington County Pennsylvania at the house of one Joseph Mills and there he was kept stationed during the whole of his said tour assisting the erection of a fort or station for the protection & safety of the citizens of that vicinity who were exposed to the hostile incursions of the Indians who about that time had become exceedingly troublesome. That during his said tour he was several times absent for a short time from the fort on small scouting and spying parties against the Indians but that he was during the principal part of said time at work on the said fort. He states that he thus continued in the service till the expiration of his said tour of duty which happened about the first of August in the year 1777. He states that he was not under the command of any field officer during this tour. That the country was a frontier thinly inhabited and the settlements mostly made within the period of a few years and according to his present best recollection there was but little sys-

tem observed at that time in the militia regulations there. That those who were able to bear arms within the circle of his acquaintance in that part of the country were under the direction and control of Capt. Williamson who made calls upon them whenever the settlements required defence from the hostile Indians.

He further states and declares that the danger from the Indians continued to increase instead of diminishing and that immediately upon the expiration of his abovenamed tour to wit in the early part of the month of August in the year 1777 he again entered the service of the United States as a militia man under the Command of Capt. David Williamson and was continued in the office of orderly sergeant to his said company. That this tour was for one month and immediately after he entered upon it he was detached from the fort at Joseph Wells' with ten or 12 men (privates) under the command of lieut. John Jones to a fort at Richard Wells's situated on Cross Creek about seven miles below the fort at Jos. Wells's where he was stationed during the whole of his said tour as a guard to the fort. That upon the expiration of his said tour of one month he was not discharged but was again called on to perform another tour of one month.

And he further states and declares that he did in conformity to said call, in the early part of the month of Septr. in the year 1777 again enter the service of the United States as a drafted militia man under the command of Capt. David Williamson upon a tour of one month. That he was still continued in the office of orderly sergeant to his company and being at the time at the fort at Jos. Wells's on Cross Creek he was detached from thence with 15 or 20 men the whole under the command of Lieut. John Jones to Cox's fort at the mouth of Cross Creek in Virginia where he remained stationed except when absent on scouting parties during the whole of the said tour of one month and was then discharged and returned to his place of residence in the said county of Washington Penn.

Like Isaac Ellis, Adam Link returned to his family farm at the end of his tour, or tours, of service. While serving at Fort Dement he certainly spent time at routine garrison duties, maintaining and improving the fort, mounting guard, moving and caring for provisions and stores, and tending to his clothing and accoutrements. He may have ventured from the fort with scouting parties, escorted supplies to or from the garrison, pursued raiders, or participated in innumerable other activities; in his depositions to the pension office, though, he mentioned no specific operations. In 1778 he was drafted again, this time serving from April 1 to October 1 at another outpost called Shepherd's Fort.[9] The following year saw another six-month tour, this time in the garrison at Wheeling; the fort there, Fort Henry, had been besieged in 1777 and depredations had been frequent in the region.[10] In dutifully recounting his service record to pension examiners, however, Link gave only dates, places, and names of officers, with no detail at all about incidents and expeditions that he witnessed or took part in.

The teenaged militiaman was noticed by his officers. Before marching out in 1778, Captain Samuel Mason, Link's company commander that year, told an acquaintance that "as Link was a good marksman he would have an opportunity to try his skill against the Indians."[11] And yet we do not know if he ever fired a shot in anger. In spite of his omission of specific events, however, Adam Link's depositions provide a vivid if brief look at the horrid warfare that he experienced. The frontier war was largely one of raids and reprisals. Indians singled out homes of settlers, killed or kidnapped the inhabitants, and burned buildings and stores. As homesteaders, Link's family was in constant danger, "very much exposed to invasion from the British and the Indians." After his first tour of militia service, Link claims to have "acted as an Indian Spy and scout" and to have spent most of his time actively engaged on the frontier. The term "Indian spy" was used liberally by many pensioners when referring to patrols undertaken to discover dispositions and movements of their opponents.[12] Link related vividly, although choppily, the harsh and dangerous conditions in which

9. A fort at present-day Elm Grove, West Virginia, named for Colonel David Shepherd of the Pennsylvania Militia.

10. Louise Phelps Kellogg, ed., *Frontier Retreat on the Upper Ohio, 1779–1781* (Madison: Wisconsin Historical Society, 1917), 54–58.

11. The acquaintance was a man named Frederick Soulzer who corroborated Link's service record, recounting having seen Link march out for service and having spoken with Captain Mason; Soulzer's deposition is in Adam Link's pension file. Pension file of Adam Link, S. 1771, Revolutionary War Pensions.

12. See, for example, the deposition of William Wolfe, S. 24020, Revolutionary War Pensions, who said that "We were all engaged as 'Indian Spies' traversing the country."

Photograph of Adam Link by Messrs. N. A. and R. A. Moore, 1864; notice the differences from the image at the end of this chapter. (*Library of Congress*)

he lived, fleeing homes with family, friends, and neighbors when raids were imminent to find shelter in log huts, local forts, or even sleeping in caves or the woods. He served in the military for only eighteen months, but spent fully four years at war. Even if he exaggerated his experiences, there can be no doubt that his adolescence and early adulthood saw much hardship and desperation.

The family farm included substantial numbers of sheep, hogs, and cattle as well as corn and other grain crops. It required work to maintain and vigilance to protect. While militia service was compulsory and contributed to safety of the region, it deprived the farm of crucial labor. When young Adam was drafted for the third time and marched off in 1779, "Link's father complained that two of his sons were now in the army when he needed them at home to help him in his business." And yet the militia could do only so much; their adversaries were skilled at stealth and surprise, and the local forts provided a safe escape for families but not protection for their far-flung farms. In spite of warnings, Adam Link's father was determined to continue working his land unintimidated by the threat of destruction. In August 1780, a summer when Adam Link was not called for service, the farm was attacked, the house, barn, and stores burned, the livestock killed or scattered. They lost everything, and worst of all, the senior Link was carried off, scalped, and killed. Now fatherless, Adam and his brother were forced to work at day labor to support their mother and sisters; if they did any additional service for the army, it was in an informal capacity.

After the war Adam Link married a relative named Elizabeth Link; in 1820 they moved from Washington County into Ohio. He was granted a pension in 1834, but soon after it was stopped by the pension office on the grounds that his claim was fraudulent. It appears that "a little strife" had arisen between Link and another unidentified person, and that person engaged a "scoundrel" lawyer to debase Link's claim of Revolutionary War service. The lawyer convinced the pension office that Link was younger than he had stated and had served only in the 1790s. The lawyer was later found to be a fraud and "escaped the penalty of the law by flight," but in the meantime Link's original pension claim was lost. For reasons that are not clear, perhaps because he was a simple frontier settler who lacked the means to engage his own lawyer or mount an organized effort, Link spent the next nineteen years eking out his own existence without the benefit of his pension.[13]

---

13. All of the documents associated with the pension's stoppage and reinstatement are in Link's pension file, but the details of the case are nonetheless difficult to piece together.

In 1851 some acquaintances brought the case to the pension department, asserting that Link was "now and has been for a long time much decrepid" and at "about 90 years of age and very infirm, not able to provide his living by his industry." Link gave another deposition in early 1852, this time showing the effects of clouding memory when compared to the deposition of two decades before. His benefits were reinstated, albeit at a reduced rate because the pension office determined that the Pennsylvania militia had never been called out for the six-month tours that Link described. If Link had overstated his service, it probably was not with intent to deceive: he had lived in a region where military service and day-to-day existence sometimes blurred together, where men responded to the behest of local leaders rather than government policy, where inhabitants "turned out" when the community was threatened and went home again when the danger subsided just as men all over the colonies had done from the first day of hostilities. He probably spent a lot of his time in the forts and garrisons when he was not formally engaged in the militia. When he was discharged from each term of service, he may not have walked right home again, but stayed in the military environment for as long as it suited him. He clearly states that he never received any written discharge, showing disregard for formality and naiveté about the future value of such documents.[14] Others gave depositions that were similar in nature to his, stating similar terms of service irrespective of the prevailing militia laws; they could not have foreseen the need for careful documentation decades in the future.

Rev. Hillard never had the opportunity to meet Adam Link; the old veteran died before the interviewer reached his Ohio homestead. Hillard's discussion of Link is, therefore, brief, consisting only of a biographical sketch and a few anecdotes related by the photographer who, fortunately, did have the opportunity to capture images. Only one detail of military service is related by Hillard, that Link was a companion to Andrew Poe, a soldier who had gained some fame for his exploits fighting the Indians. Such an association is wholly unverified; Link's pension depositions make

14. According to pension depositions of many who served in the Pennsylvania militia, few if any received discharge documents.

no mention of Poe, and the pension deposition of Andrew Poe's brother Adam gives no suggestion that the Poe brothers ever served in the same military units that Link did.[15] They were certainly in the same region, but there is no evidence that they were ever at the same location; the incidents for which Andrew Poe became most famous, and to which Hillard alludes in vague terms, occurred in 1781, two years after Link's last militia service.[16] A connection between the two men is plausible, but we lack any direct evidence except Hillard's assertion. Hillard's account of Link's life subsequent to the Revolution is accurate in that it correlates with information in the pension files. Very little else is known about this veteran who spent the remainder of his long life in the hardscrabble existence of a frontier farmer, first in his native Pennsylvania and then in Ohio.

Considering that Link was photographed "without his knowledge" when Nelson Augustus Moore visited him, it is remarkable that the photographer was able to capture four distinct images of the old man. Publication of *The Last Men of the Revolution* initiated a period of posthumous fame for Adam Link. In 1885 an Arizona newspaper published a biography of him, mostly paraphrased directly from the book. It includes, however, a unique passage that gives a bit more insight into the constitution of this man who spent his life on the frontier and his teen years as a warrior:

> As years grew upon him in his lonely widowed condition, he went to live with his son-in-law, Horatio Markley, in Crawford county, with whom he spent his last years.
>
> Mr. Link was often remonstrated with by Mr. Markley about his constant use of whisky; he said, in reply, "Well, if you will quit smoking I will quit whisky." Mr. M. being an inveterate smoker could not undertake this; but, after being prostrated by sickness, upon his convalescence, he says: "I have quit smoking." Never a drop of spirituous liquor passed the lips of Adam Link again, being 90 years of age. The life long slavish habit had such a hold

15. Pension deposition of Adam Poe, R. 8292, Revolutionary War Pensions.

16. The stories of Andrew Poe and his brother Adam were investigated by historian Lyman C. Draper; letters between Draper and Andrew Poe's son from 1849 and 1852 are in the Draper Manuscripts, Wisconsin Historical Society, Series NN.

upon him that he was prostrated, and was so near death that all thought he must die, and all knew the remedy, and none better than the old hero himself; but no, his word had been given. He recovered and was in his last years better for it.[17]

17. *Arizona Champion*, March 14, 1885.

Like most other militiamen, it is unlikely that Adam Link was issued a military uniform when he served in the Pennsylvania militia on the western frontier in 1777, 1778, and 1779. The region had seen frequent armed conflict even before the Revolutionary War, however, as settlers pushed native inhabitants off their tribal lands. The settlers may have been better acclimated to extended periods of military service than militias closer to the coast that had practiced only on occasional weekends. There was, nonetheless, probably little difference between the clothing these frontiersmen wore for working their farms and for serving in the militia.

The soldier seen here is marching out for a tour away from home that could well extend long past the stipulated two-month duration. He wears a knapsack to carry a few extra shirts, stockings, shoes, and other necessities; above this is a blanket rolled around a tumpline. In addition to his cartridge pouch, he has a tomahawk (with no protective covering for its sharp blade) and a wooden canteen; his American-made musket is designed for hunting and has no provision for affixing a bayonet. His black felt hat is modern and fashionable, showing a strong attachment to the European style of civilization being pushed deeper into the American frontier. Knowing that most of his time will be spent in the small forts built to protect each settlement, he wears no gaiters or leggings. Firearms of military quality were always in short supply; whether Adam Link received a musket from the state or used one that was in his family is not known.

For more on civilian clothing in the frontier region, see Ellen J. Gehert, *Rural Pennsylvania Clothing: Being a Study of the Wearing Apparel of the German and English Inhabitants Both Men and Women, who Resided in Southeastern Pennsylvania in the Late Eighteenth and Early Nineteenth Century* (York, PA: Liberty Cap Books, 1976); and Thomas Verenna, "A Want of Arms in Pennsylvania," Journal of the American Revolution, April 24, 2014, allthingsliberty.com/2014/04/a-want-of-arms-in-pennsylvania/.

Drawing by Eric H. Schnitzer

The Pension Depositions of Adam Link[18]

1833

On this 25 day of Septr. in the year one thousand eight hundred and thirty three, personally appeared before Wells Kellogg Esquire a Justice of the Peace Adam Link a resident of the Township of Milton, in the County of Richland and State of Ohio, aged seventy two years who being first duly sworn according to law doth on his oath make the following declaration in order to obtain the benefit of the provision made by the act of Congress passed June 7th 1832. That he entered the service of the Revolutionary War in the year one thousand seven hundred and seventy seven on the first of month of June of said year, and served under Captain Williamson[19] in the Militia of the State of Pennsylvania for a period of six months, and said Williamson his Captain was, during said tour, promoted to be a Colonel in said Militia, and then this applicant was commanded by one Captain Biggs,[20] and said tour of service were sent to keep garrison at a place called "Dement's Fort,"[21] and this applicant cannot now recollect the number of the regiment to which the company he served in belonged, that Williamson was Colonel of the regiment, and this deponent further says that he is not able now to recollect the name of the Colonel who commanded the regiment before the promotion of said Capt. Williamson. That he entered and served from the first of June 1777 and served until the first of December 1777. That he served as above in the capacity of a private soldier for said period, when he was verbally dismissed from the service, but never received any written evidence of his services from said officers, that he was drafted out to serve in the County of Washington in said State.

18. Pension depositions of Adam Link, S. 1771, Revolutionary War Pensions. Although the original 1833 documents were lost, copies of them are in the pension file.

19. Captain, later Lieutenant Colonel, David Williamson of the Pennsylvania militia.

20. Captain John Biggs of the Pennsylvania Militia; he was killed in the Sandusky expedition in May 1782.

21. The quotation marks around many names are in the original manuscript in the pension file.

And this applicant further states that he again served as a private soldier in the Revolutionary Army another tour of six months in the militia of the State of Pennsylvania, that he drafted to serve said period in Washington County in said State–that he entered the service under one Captain Mason, and was placed under the command of Colonel Williamson, that he entered in the Spring of the year one thousand seven hundred and seventy eight in the month of April, that he served from the 1st of April until the first of October in the said year 1778–that the number of the regiment he does not recollect–that the troops were sent to a place called Shepherd's Fort, where they were stationed to keep charge of the garrison at said place during the time said tour of six months under the said officers above named, where he received a verbal dismissal from the service, but received no written discharge from his officers–that he so entered the service in the County of Washington in the State of Pennsylvania–and this applicant further states that he again entered the service for a third period of six months in the County of Washington in the State of Pennsylvania, that he served in the Militia of said State for a period of six months as a drafted militiaman under one Captain Noble and the Lieutenant's name was "Ogle"[22] and the Colonel's name was "Shepherd"[23]–that he entered the service in the County of Washington and marched from said County into the State of Virginia to a place called "Wheeling Garrison" where they served this tour of duty at said place under said officers. That he entered the service this last time on the 15th of June in the year 1779, and served until the 20th of December thereafter, making this last tour of Revolutionary service of six months under said officers above named when he was verbally dismissed from the service by his officers, but never received any written discharge from his services–and that I was not during my eighteen months service engaged at any time in civil pursuits–that this applicant has no written evidence of his discharge or services in the Revolutionary War. That he is now old, weak and infirm, and is not, in consequence of impaired memory,

22. Captain Noble and Lieutenant Ogle have not been identified; both surnames appear with some frequency on records from the region, but no muster rolls of the corps in which Link served have been found.

23. Colonel David Shepherd of the Pennsylvania militia.

able at this time to recollect all the particulars of his service, but the above is as particular as he is able at this time to recollect—and this applicant says he is not now able to prove his services or any part or portion of them by any contemporary survivor of the revolutionary War, other than by the annexed deposition herewith exhibited. That the soldiers who served with this applicant are now dead or reside in parts not known at this time to the applicant, and cannot be had or procured to prove the services of this applicant. The names of the officers who served with me were Captain Mason, Captain Noble and Captain Biggs—Lieutenant "Ogle," Colonel Williamson and Colonel Shepherd.

I the said Adam Link do hereby relinquish every claim whatever to a pension or annuity except the present, and he declares that his name is not on the pension Roll of any Agency in any State.

1. Where and in what year were you born?

Answer. I was born in the year 1760, in the State of Pennsylvania.

2. Have you any record of your age, & if so where is it?

Answer. I have no record of my age, my father had one, but it is lost or destroyed long since, it is out of my power to produce it—my father kept my age in an old family Bible which is now lost & destroyed.

3. Where were you living when called into service, where have you lived since the Revolutionary War, and where do you now live?

Answer. I lived at the time I was called into service, in Washington County, in the State of Pennsylvania, and since the Revolutionary War, I have resided about seven years in the County of Beaver in the State of Pennsylvania and then I removed into the state of Ohio where I now live.

4. How were you called into service? Were you drafted, did you volunteer, or were you a substitute? And if a substitute, for whom?

Answer. I was three times drafted out to serve in the militia of the State of Pennsylvania for three terms of six months each, making a Revolutionary service of one year and six months, and that the same was served by me as a private Soldier.

5. State the names of the officers under whom you served.

My Captains was Mason, Captain Noble, Captain Biggs, & Lieutenant "Ogle"—Colonels names were Williamson and Colonel Shepherd.

I Adam Link applicant for a pension who has subscribed & sworn to the annexed declaration further states that in the war of the revolution my parents resided in Washington County in Pennsylvania near the line of the State of Virginia, that our family suffered severely in the war, that the Indians murdered & scalped my father in the war, burned his house & barn & took away all his stock of cattle & horses, & forced my father & family to leave their home with all the corn & crops standing on the land, my father was a man not to be intimidated by the Indians and was often cautioned that he would be butchered, but he always insisted that he would stand his ground & not go away for any Indian or any enemy, but he was at length killed by the Indians in the year 1780. I served one year and six months, and so did my brother (who is now dead) serve in the war of the Revolution as I have stated & set forth in my amended declaration, and I do further state that residing as we did in that part of the State of Pennsylvania & situated where we were, no family could suffer more in distress & cruelty than did my father & his family. We had often to unite in neighborhoods & go & lie in small bodies of men & get into some old log building and stand with our guns in our hands to defend the lives of our sisters & friends until the Indians had dispersed & that I do say that we were all surrounded with Butchers, death & cruelty where we lived, all was "war and death," we fled sometimes to our neighbors, sometimes to the woods, & at other times to the Forts & garrisons for protection of their lives, & in fact I was almost continually in service of my country through the most of the revolutionary war as volunteer at short intervals to aid in defending the Western Frontiers with the rest of my friends & neighbors who resided in that part of the State, but was only three times drafted for six months each, making regular service as a drafted militia man for eighteen months as a private soldier. I would further mention that Captain Mason who commanded me as mentioned in my declaration hereto annexed was shot through the hips at Wheeling garrison by a musket or rifle ball by an Indian while lying at the garrison.

1852

The State of Ohio Ashland County: On this Eleventh day of February in the year of our Lord one thousand eight hundred and fifty two personally appeared before me J. A. McClusky a Justice of the peace in and for the County of Ashland and State of Ohio, Adam Link, a resident of the said County of Ashland and State of Ohio, aged Eighty-Eight years, who being first duly sworn, according to law, doth on his oath say, and makes the following declaration, in order to obtain the benefit of the provisions made by the act of Congress passed June the seventh A. D. Eighteen hundred and thirty two,

That he was a Soldier in the revolutionary war with Great Britain; that in the month of March seventeen hundred and seventy five he settled at the place called Middle Wheeling on the Ohio River, and that in the summer of the year A.D. seventeen hundred and seventy seven I was stationed in Sheppards fort, and helped to garrison and defend the fort for five months. Affiant further says that by reason of his old age and the consequent loss of his memory he cannot now swear positively as to the precise dates, nor the precise length of time he was in one fort, or served as an Indian Spy but will endeavor to give all as near as he can. And he further says that after he with his company left fort Shepperd in the fall of seventeen hundred and seventy seven he acted as an Indian Spy and scout, and was actually engaged along the frontier until the summer of seventeen hundred and seventy eight, when he was again called upon to garrison and defend Dements fort for five months. After our discharge from the last named fort I was again continually engaged as an Indian Spy until the following year when if my memory serves me right we were again placed in Dements fort, but how long we remained there at that time I cannot certainly tell. In the year A.D. seventeen hundred and eighty, in the month of August our house was burned by the Indians, and my father was taken prisoner, and our house was then burnt to ashes, and everything we had in it destroyed, our barn was burnt, and about forty head of sheep burnt up with it, all our horses and cattle were driven off and killed, and about one hundred head of hogs destroyed, and totally lost; and my father was marched out a few miles by the Indians, and murdered and scalped, we also had three hundred bushels of grain burnt by the Indians and a large field of corn entirely destroyed. Although we had a large property at that time, I and my eldest brother were then compelled to work days work for our support, and the maintenance of our mother and sisters. In the year A.D. seventeen hundred and eighty two[24] I was again stationed in Moore's fort in Washington County Pennsylvania for the term of six months as near as I can now remember or from the spring until the fall of the year. In the year A.D. eighteen hundred and ninety[25] as near as I can now remember the time I volunteered in the company commanded by Captain Noble to join St. Clair's Army[26] but from some cause was never called on to go, although I stood ready to march, at a moments warning. From the commencement of the Revolutionary war, almost until its close I was continually on the frontier, and exposed to all the hardships, and dangers, and privations of a border warfare, and a frontier life; I have lived for days and nights lied in a cave of rocks, to save my life from the merciless savages. I was for more than four years from the commencement of the Revolutionary war continually engaged either in garrisoning forts, or serving as an Indian Spy; or defending the frontier settlements with whatever of skill, and courage I could command.

Perhaps more than fifteen years since I made my application to the Pension Office for a pension and sent on the proofs, in the same was held to be sufficient; and a pension was allowed to me, and my pension was then again stopped and as I have been informed through the representations of persons wholly ignorant both of my past life and my services to my country, and that I had an Original Pension certificate issued by the Commissioner of Pensions to me, for a long time in my possession and that if my memory has not failed may I gave it Judge Patterson who was at that time a member of Congress from this District, and that after diligent search it cannot now be found. And I hereby relinquish any claim whatever to a pension or annuity except the present and

24. Link's third tour was actually in 1779, as stated in his previous deposition.
25. Clearly this is a transcription error or a slip of the tongue, and should be 1790 rather than 1890.
26. The army under Major General Arthur St. Clair that fought in Ohio in 1790 and 1791.

declare that my name is not on the pension roll of the agency of any state.

Adam Link, his mark[27]

1855

State of Ohio

County of Ashland

On this 21st day of April A.D. one thousand eight hundred and fifty five personally appeared before me J. A. McClusky Esqr. Within and for the County and state aforesaid Adam Link aged 92 years a resident of Ashland county in the State of Ohio who being duly sworn according to law declares that he is the identical Adam Link who was a soldier in the Revolutionary war commenced April 1775 ended November 1783 in the company commanded by Captain David Williamson in the Regiment of Virginia Militia commanded by Col. Shepard, that he enlisted at Wheeling or Shepard fort Va on or about the 20th day of May A.D. 1777 for the term of six month and continued in actual service in said war for the term of ten months and was honorably discharged on the 20th day of May A.D. 1778.

He makes this declaration for the purpose of obtaining the bounty land to which he may be entitled under the act approved March 1, 1855, he also declares that he has not received a warrant for bounty land under this or any other act of Congress, nor made any other application therefore. The claimant draws a pension from the Department at this time.

Adam Link, his mark

27. This document, and the 1855 document, have Link's name written in the same hand as the rest of the text; an X is scrawled between the first and last name, with "his" written above the X and "mark" below it.

RESIDENCE of ADAM LINK.

LITH. OF BINGHAM & DODD, HARTFORD, CT.

Lithograph of Adam Link's home, Summer 1864, from *Last Men of the Revolution*. (*Society of the Cincinnati*)

Adam Link

From E. B. Hillard, *The Last Men of the Revolution* (1864)

THE NAME OF ADAM LINK INTRODUCES THE CLOSING SKETCH OF the pensioners of the Revolution. Since his picture was taken, he, also, has passed away by death.

He was born in Washington county, near Hagerstown, Maryland, November 14, 1761. He died at Sulphur Springs, Crawford county, Ohio, August 15, 1864. His age was one hundred and two years, nine months, and one day.

The circumstances of Mr. Link's life were humble, and his part in the war unimportant. He enlisted at the age of sixteen, in Wheeling, Virginia, for the frontier service, and spent five years in that service, most in the vicinity of Wheeling. During this time, his father, Jacob Link, was murdered by the Indians in his own house. Mr. Link was in no important battle of the war. The only interesting circumstance of his soldier life was his companionship with Poe, the famous Indian hunter, the incident of whose meeting with the Indian chief upon the shore of the lake whither both had withdrawn from the fight, to wash out their guns, (become foul through use)—Poe completing first the cleansing of his, and so gaining the first shot, which brought down the Indian, and saved his own life,— is familiar.

At the age of twenty-eight years, he married Elizabeth Link, a distant relative of his, her age being seventeen. After this event, being fond of change, he roamed about from place to place, living but a short time in each; and so spent the earlier part of his life. At the age of sixty, he walked from his home in Pennsylvania to Ohio, a distance of one hundred and forty-one miles, accomplishing it in three days, an average of forty-seven miles a day. When seventy years of age, he set about clearing a farm, living the while in a

Adam Link, photographed by Messrs. N. A. and R. A. Moore, 1864.
(*Society of the Cincinnati*)

house the main wall of which was formed by the flat roots of an upturned tree. Although always a hard worker, he was always poor, the account of which his habits, which were always irregular, partly furnish and part may be set down to the score of that ill luck which seems to dog the steps of some men through life. However, he cleared quite a farm after passing the limit of three score years and ten, and remained for some time on it. Finally, he went to live with his son-in-law in Crawford county, Ohio, where he resided until his death.

Perpetuating the habits of the frontier service, Mr. Link roughed it through life. His constitution must have been of iron to have endured his irregularities and excesses. He paid no attention to his manner of eating, either in quantity, quality, or time; and he was addicted to strong drink. He labored severely and constantly. Notwithstanding all, his health was good till near the very close of his life. A few years before, during a severe thunder storm, his sight was strangely affected by the lightning. For a long time, everything appeared distorted and askew; men had bent legs and bodies, chickens were twisted out of shape, and the keyhole of his trunk tormented him by the figures which it assumed. From this affection, however, he recovered, though never so as again to read. A short time before his death, he suffered a stroke of paralysis, which deprived him of the use of his limbs to some extent, and made his utterance difficult. However, it left his hearing good and his intellect unimpaired. Upon the artist (at his visit for the purpose of procuring his picture) telling him that he had come a long way to see him, he replied, "You can see me cheap now. Whatever else," he continued, "they may say of me, no man ever could call me a coward." He has persistently refused to have his picture taken–that given in this series being secured without his knowledge; the family fearing the proposal would provoke him, and thus defeat the attempt. In politics, Mr. Link declared himself a "Jeffersonian Democrat;" though his last vote was Republican. He said but little about the present war, frequently forgetting that one was in progress, and when reminded of it, he failed altogether to comprehend it. One of his great-grand-sons is in the army.

At the writing of this sketch, he is the last of the survivors of the Revolution known to have died.

Conclusion

From E. B. Hillard, *The Last Men of the Revolution* (1864)

JAMES BARHAM. THIS IS THE NAME OF A SOLDIER OF THE Revolution—one of the twelve surviving pensioners reported by the Commissioner of Pensions to Congress in February last—of whom it is not known whether he is living or dead. All that is known of him is, that he is recorded in the General Pension Office as "on the St. Louis, Missouri, roll, at $32.33 per annum; born in Southampton county, Virginia, May 18, 1764; age, 100 years and 7 months;" and that he was reported by the St. Louis Pension Agency, in March last, as at that time residing in Greene county, in that state.[1]

Endeavor has been made to find him and procure his photograph and a sketch of his life, but thus far without success. As no intelligence, however, has been received at the Pension Office of his death, the hope may be indulged that he is still living.

All the remaining pensioners included in the Commissioner's report are known to be dead.

These, then, are the Last Men of the Revolution:

SAMUEL DOWNING,	WILLIAM HUTCHINGS,
ALEXANDER MILLINER,	LEMUEL COOK,
DANIEL WALDO,	ADAM LINK,
JAMES BARHAM.	

1. See the Epilogue for more on James Barham.

As we name them, our thoughts recall those other seven men, the first of the great series of which these are the last: Jonas Parker, Isaac Muzzey, Jonathan Harrington, Caleb Harrington, Robert Monroe, Samuel Hadley, John Brown.[2]

Those–the men of Lexington–opened the roll of devotion and glory; these close it. How grand a roll! How signal the period which these names respectively inaugurate and conclude! How great and how important a part of the world's history do these lives embrace! How vast they seem,–the lives of individuals, yet commensurate with an epoch in the life of the race! To the student of history there is profound satisfaction in such living connection of one of its great periods with another. The lover of his country will even recognize a favoring Providence in the signal prolongation of their lives–so far beyond the ordinary limit of human existence–as though it were that the first great conflict of the national development might, through its living representatives, impart its sanction and transmit its inspiration to the second.

But from these more general reflections we turn, in closing, to the men. And well we may; for while the lessons which their lives teach us will remain with us, they themselves will soon be gone. Already their loneliness affects with tender pathos our hearts,–so far away from what to them were life and friends,–so few of all once comrades in battle and victory!

> *The ranks are thin, and wide*
> *Apart in the dim armies of the past;*
> *Faint and afar they stand, who side by side*
> *Their steel-clamped columns on the foemen cast.*
> *In the still camp of death*
> *The comrades of their toils and triumphs lie;*
> *And marble sentries guard with noiseless breath*
> *Their green encampments of Eternity.*

But before they pass to join those far encampments, we rejoice to pay them the tribute of a nation's gratitude and honor. We honor them in the significance (now through like experience perceived anew) of the great conflict in which they bore a part, and of which they stand to us the representatives. Nor to us alone. For as

---

2. These are the men who died in Lexington, Massachusetts, on April 19, 1775 in the skirmish that began the war.

the Revolution was an event, not in American history only, but in the history of the world,—since the rights contended for in it were "the rights of human nature,"—so these few humble men, its alone survivors, are objects of the liveliest interest—the most sacred regard to every lover of liberty throughout the world. They stand forth in all their lowliness to all lands and nations and times; the representatives of that great movement in human history which vindicated liberty as possible to and the right of all.

With this distinction we may leave them, rejoicing to see how time, over all earthly circumstance, at last crowns and enthrones devotion to a good cause.

To those engaged in the preparation of this memorial, it has been a grateful service. For not only is it a rare privilege, from their historic associations, to have seen these men, but there is that in them which awakens regard, as well as excites interest. They are good old men, kindly, pleasant, Christian; waiting humbly, patiently, and hopefully till their change come. May God support and comfort their closing days! And before they close, may this brief, common record of their lives afford them gratification, as, strangers hitherto, in it they meet, as it were, together: and, comrades in the old common conflict, take each other by the hand, and look into each other's faces, and tell to one another the story of their lives, before they say the last farewell.[3]

One of these men will be the last survivor of the American Revolution. Which will it be?

How great will be the break when he is gone!

> *Be naught but ashes here*
> *That keep awhile my semblance, who was John—*
> *Still, when they scatter, there is left on earth*
> *No one alive who knew, (consider this!)*
> *Saw with his eyes, and handled with his hands,*
> *That which was from the first, the Word of Life.*
> *How will it be when none more saith, 'I saw!'"*

—Browning's *Dramatis Personæ.*

3. Here Rev. Hillard included a series of notes concerning the congressional resolution of March 4, 1864, the list of twelve pensioners thought to be alive at that time, and notices of the deaths of those who had passed away between that time and the book's publication. This information has been related in the introduction to this volume, so it has been omitted here.

Epilogue

WERE THEY THE LAST MEN? AT THE TIME REV. HILLARD MADE his rounds, they seemed to be. The veterans he visited had come to the nation's attention because they were the last surviving pensioners of the American Revolution, but it was the fact of drawing pensions that made them known: the government paid them regularly and reported the expenditure. The annual reporting of pension payments was the only record of which Revolutionary War veterans remained alive. The Moore brothers and Rev. Hillard saw a list that included twelve names, but five had passed on before they could be photographed.

There was one pensioner that neither the photographers nor Rev. Hillard could track down. James Barham was born in 1864 and served for just under ten months in the Virginia militia late in the war. By 1855 he had settled in Greene County, Missouri, but Rev. Hillard was unable to learn more about him in the war-divided country; he nonetheless included a brief statement about Barham in his book's conclusion. Barham was in fact still alive, and remained so until January 8, 1865. A tintype photograph, in poor condition, of James Barham and his son is in possession of his descendants, and is depicted in Maureen Taylor's book *The Last Muster*.[1]

---

1. Taylor, *The Last Muster Volume 2*, 22.

The year before the Moore brothers and Rev. Hillard began their pensioner project, a Boston publisher named George W. Tomlinson compiled his own list of surviving pensioners. His impetus is not known, but his results were published as a full-page item in the *New York Herald* on October 19, 1863.[2] The following year the material was released as a twenty-page pamphlet.[3] Many publications included notices of it at the same time that they mentioned *The Last Men of the Revolution.* Tomlinson identified twenty-three pensioners including the twelve cited by Congress in March 1864. He arrived at this greater number primarily because he included men residing in states that had seceded from the Union—men who were no longer receiving pensions not because they were known to have died but because they were not, at the time, under the governance of the United States. His efforts suffered from the same information latency as Hillard's; several of the men had died before the pamphlet was published, and the remainder died within the next year or two.[4]

The sudden popularity of these last pensioners, brought about not so much by the book and photographs but by widespread newspaper coverage, raised the question of whether there were other survivors who were not on the pension rolls. There were claims and rumors, but with the nation divided and disrupted by the Civil War it was difficult to authenticate them. When hostilities ended, by which time several of the known pensioners had died, it became feasible to verify all of the claims and search the nation more thoroughly for others. By 1866 it became apparent that several men were yet alive who had legitimate claims as veterans of

2. *New York Herald*, October 19, 1863. The article bears no byline, but contains the same material as the octavo pamphlet published the following year. Tomlinson published the pamphlet but there is no direct indication of who actually compiled the information.

3. *The Old Roll of Fame: The Patriots of the Revolution of '76* (Boston: G. W. Tomlinson, 1864). The 1863 newspaper item bore the same title.

4. Of the eleven men identified by Tomlinson but not included in the 1864 congressional resolution, eight are known to have died by the end of 1864. Three dates of death have not been found: John Brooks, born in Bladen County, North Carolina, circa 1757; James Copeland, born in Cheraw District, South Carolina, circa 1764; and Henry Willoughby, born in Virginia circa 1761; no information about any of these men was reported after the Civil War ended, so it is reasonable to conclude that they had died by 1865.

the now-distant war. They had in years past filed claims for pensions, but were rejected because their service did not fall within the scope of the pension acts.

John Gray was born in Fairfax County, Virginia, in the first days of January 1764. He joined the army in 1781 but served just three months in a Virginia militia company; a month after his discharge he joined another militia company and stayed on for five months, just long enough to be present at the British surrender at Yorktown. It was not until 1855 that he entered a claim for a pension, "not having served for sufficient time to entitle me to a Pension under existing Laws."[5] He had long since moved from Virginia to Ohio and lived an austere and obscure life. But once awareness of the last surviving pensioners spread across the nation, his name was brought to the forefront. His photograph was taken; a copy of it appears in *The Last Muster.*[6] As other pensioners died off, national awareness of Gray as one of the Revolution's last survivors brought about a special act of Congress to grant him a pension. House bill No. 1044 "for the relief of John Gray" was passed in February 1867 by the 39th Congress, awarding Gray an annual pension of five hundred dollars. By this time the only other remaining pensioner was Samuel Downing, whose pension was increased to the same amount.

John Gray's newfound popularity led to a biography being written by a long-time neighbor of his, James M. Dalzell.[7] Dalzell admitted, however, the challenge he faced in chronicling the old veteran's life: "Only from his lips could I gather up the raveled thread of his life. To him, therefore, I went, and to his neighbors; and from them gleaned the fragmentary points presented in this volume." For this very reason, *John Gray, of Mount Vernon; The Last Soldier of the Revolution* suffers from the same issues as Rev. Hillard's biographical sketches of six other veterans. Dalzell's book claims that "Mr. Gray's father enlisted in 1777, and fell at White Plains," a battle that occurred in 1776. That Gray "had been one of Washington's favorite soldiers," but his short service in the Virginia

5. Pension file of John Gray, S. 1464, Revolutionary War Pensions.

6. Taylor, *The Last Muster*, 68.

7. James M. Dalzell, *John Gray, of Mount Vernon: The Last Soldier of the Revolution* (Washington, DC: Gibson Brothers, 1868).

militia could have put him in close proximity to Washington only briefly, if at all. Dalzell admits that "Mr. Gray had grown quite infirm, and could hardly hear us speaking. His memory, of course, had somewhat failed. So this may account for some discrepancies in this book." The discrepancies of verifiable facts, though, make it difficult to judge the veracity of the personal anecdotes and other unverifiable material in the account.

John Gray died on March 29, 1868, at 104 years of age. But he was not the last survivor of the American Revolution. Another man had also come to light.

In western New York, a man of German descent named Daniel Frederick Bakeman had resided without a pension because he had no proof of his service during the Revolutionary War. He had served for perhaps four years in Lieutenant Colonel Marinus Willett's Regiment of New York Levies on the frontier; part of that time was spent at Fort Plain in New York, where he may have crossed paths with Samuel Downing. Bakeman had lost all records of his service, apparently in a house fire.[8] As with John Gray, Bakeman's case was brought before Congress and he, too, was awarded a pension by the special act of February 1867. He was photographed, and the picture was reproduced in *carte de visite* prints for widespread distribution.[9] Bakeman lived until April 5, 1869, over six months after reaching the age of 109. Because of the 1867 act of Congress, Bakeman was indisputably the last pensioner of the American Revolution.

There were, however, long-lived veterans of the war who were not pensioners. John Phillips, lifelong resident of Sturbridge, Massachusetts, joined a militia company on December 10, 1776, when he was sixteen years old. He spent the next six weeks in Providence, Rhode Island, keeping a watch on the British force that had just occupied nearby Newport.[10] When his short term of service was up, he refused an appointment to corporal and instead

8. Pension file of Daniel Frederick Bakeman, S. 17265, Revolutionary War Pensions.

9. Taylor, *The Last Muster*, 27.

10. Pension file of John Phillips, B. L. Wt. 75036-160-55, Revolutionary War Pensions. His deposition claims seven weeks, but an affidavit in the file states that his name appears on a pay roll as having served from December 10, 1776, until January 20, 1777.

returned to his hometown where, in August 1856, a biographer recorded the story of his life and he sat for a daguerreotype photograph.[11] He died in February 1865, four months short of his 105th birthday. James Allen had enlisted as a fifer in the Connecticut militia in September 1782, shortly before his fourteenth birthday, and served "till the news of peace in 1783."[12] He was unable to claim a pension in 1818 because he was not in Continental service, and when he tried again in 1832 he was unable to prove his service with documents or witnesses. He made another attempt in 1858 in Maine where he then resided, but to no avail; his inability to provide sufficient proof of his service caused his claim to once more be rejected. He had his photograph taken, and lived until May 5, 1867.[13]

Neither of these men, nor indeed any of the pensioners, surpassed John Kitts, who lived into his 108th year in 1870. He was brought to the attention of the 41st Congress that year when bill H.R. 1192 was sent to the Committee on Revolutionary Pensions requesting that he be added to the rolls (which by this time included only widows and other eligible dependents).[14] No action was taken on the bill, however; this is perhaps because facts about the actual service of Kitts are elusive. A soldier by this name served in the Pennsylvania militia and applied for a pension in 1832, but that man clearly stated that he was born in March 1756.[15] The John Kitts alive in 1870 came suddenly to national attention in 1867, and the many newspaper accounts published from then through his passing generally reported that he was born in 1762. They claim that he served in the 1st Pennsylvania Regiment when he was just fourteen years old, that he bore the mark of a musket ball wound on the back of his head received during the siege of Yorktown in October 1781, and that he witnessed the surrender of Cornwallis.[16]

11. F. W. Emmons, *The Biography and Phrenological Character of Deacon John Phillips: with the addresses, poem, and original hymns, of the celebration of his One-Hundredth Birthday* (Southbridge, MA: O. D. Haven, 1860); Taylor, *The Last Muster Volume 2*, 78.

12. Pension file of James Allen, R. 12085, Revolutionary War Pensions.

13. Taylor, *The Last Muster*, 18–19.

14. Journals of the House of Representatives, February 10 and 12, 1870.

15. Pension file of John Kitts, S. 23745, Revolutionary War Pensions.

16. See, for example, *Ohio Democrat*, September 13, 1867, and *New York Herald*, February 11, 1870.

At this writing, however, no muster rolls or other records have been found to corroborate this. Several men named John Kitts participated in the war, but none has been definitively linked to the man who lived until September 1870.[17]

There are other claims, equally if not more challenging than Kitts's, to corroborate.[18] Because of the relative certainty of the pension claims, Daniel Bakeman remains generally accepted as the last survivor, and is certainly the last surviving pensioner. Given the popularity and sudden celebrity of the pensioners listed in March 1864, the unexpected surfacing of Bakeman raised some suspicion and doubts, particularly among those who had already claimed their own local man as the last survivor. For most, the 1867 special act of Congress was convincing enough, but challenges have been made from time to time. In 1910 a pitch was made by Hon. James S. Simmons, a congressman representing a district in western New York, to declare Lemuel Cook the last survivor of the American Revolution. He directed a letter to the Bureau of Pensions requesting that they change their records, calling the 1867 special act a "shady transaction," and asserting that the claims of Bakeman, Gray, and Samuel Downing were spurious because they had not been with Washington at Yorktown. This was clearly a ploy to gain recognition for the congressman's district where Cook had lived; the Bureau of Pensions dismissed the attempt, noting that there were three veterans who outlived Cook and that "their presence at Yorktown, has no bearing upon the case as service at any period during the Revolution was considered equally honorable."[19]

Americans, of course, were not the only veterans of the American Revolution. After the death of Daniel Bakeman, a letter was sent from America to *The Times* of London inquiring whether any British army veterans of the war might still be living. The question was a plausible one: although most British soldiers enlisted in their early twenties, some did join as teenagers. Children "born in the army" could go on the muster rolls as drummers when they

17. A photograph of Kitts appears in Taylor, *The Last Muster*, 90–91.
18. See, for example, Taylor, *The Last Muster Volume 2*, 12–13.
19. Copies of the correspondence can be found in the pension files of Daniel Frederick Bakeman and Lemuel Cook.

were twelve years old.[20] While the numbers were proportionally few, it was reasonable to assume that there were a few hundred men who, if they had turned twelve in the early 1780s and managed to become centenarians, could have been alive in 1869. *The Times* published the letter and promptly received a response that a pensioner living in Bath had been a drummer in the 62nd Regiment of Foot in America and was 105 years old. A visit to this veteran and some investigation of the pension records, however, quickly affirmed that he had not been born until 1789 and therefore clearly had no involvement in the American Revolution. No other claims came forward, and the question was soon forgotten.[21]

It might be possible to determine the last surviving British army pensioner who served in America, but it would be no easy task and the results would be uncertain. At the time of the American Revolution, the British army already had a well-established pension system; soldiers who had served for twenty years or who had been disabled in the service stood a reasonably good chance of receiving a pension.[22] A set of records available today details each man's age when he received his pension, the number of years he had served, the date on which he had been awarded the pension, and the date when he died. These records, however, are organized based on the last regiment in which the man served and do not include the complete service record.[23] It is, then, possible to determine which aged pensioners were probably in the army at the time of the American Revolution, but not whether they had served in America. Tracing each man's career backward through muster

20. For details on enlistment ages of British soldiers, see Don N. Hagist, *British Soldiers, American War* (Yardley, PA: Westholme Publishing, 2012), 307n1.

21. *The Times* (London), May 11, May 14, May 18, and May 22, 1869.

22. For details on the British pension system and likelihood of Revolutionary War veterans to receive pensions, see Hagist, *British Soldiers, American War*, 182–190.

23. Royal Hospital, Chelsea: Regimental Registers of Pensioners, WO 120, British National Archives. This series extends to 1877 and records dates of death after about 1812, so the longest-lived pensioners who served in America are likely to be identifiable. But, because British soldiers often changed regiments, and sometimes did not serve continuously (that is, a man might be discharged and reenlist a few years later), there is no way to correlate the information in WO 120 with service in America.

rolls could reveal more, but gaps in muster rolls and potential gaps in any given man's service make it unlikely that a useful conclusion could be reached.[24] In the same way that the U.S. Bureau of Pensions recognized that "service at any period during the Revolution was considered equally honorable," the British pension office considered service at any period during its army's long history equally honorable and did not distinguish service in individual conflicts.

Large numbers of Americans took up arms against the rebellion, serving in the ranks of regiments raised in America for the duration of the war. These loyalist regiments were, for the most part, disbanded when hostilities ended; large numbers of men and their families took refuge in Canada rather than remain in communities where they might face hostile treatment for their support of the British government. They settled on land grants in present-day Nova Scotia, Prince Edward Island, New Brunswick, Ontario, and Quebec, where they established new lives and faced the same hardships as frontier settlers in the United States. In 1839 the New Brunswick government passed "An Act for the Relief of Old Soldiers of the Revolutionary War and their Widows."[25] Careful scrutiny of the records of those pensions could reveal the last pensioner who survived in New Brunswick, but not those who had settled in other provinces, gone to other countries, or stayed in America. Identifying the last surviving loyalist soldier is even less likely than identifying the last surviving British soldier who served in the American Revolution.

No attempt has been made by this author to investigate the last surviving German, French, or Spanish soldiers to serve in America during the Revolutionary War; each of those nationalities no doubt presents its own archival challenges. The last living man to have

24. Many regiments have gaps of one or a few years in their surviving muster rolls; those rolls are in the WO 12 collection, National Archives of Great Britain. Many soldiers had gaps in their service, having been discharged from one regiment and then joined another some years later; this is seen on many soldiers' discharges in WO 121, National Archives of Great Britain. These discharges survive only for soldiers who received pensions, but not for all soldiers who received pensions.

25. *Journal of the House of Assembly of the Province of New Brunswick* (Fredericton, NB: John Simpson, 1839).

borne arms during the American Revolution will probably never be known with any measure of certainty.

The six pensioners whom Rev. Hillard wrote about and the others photographed around the same time became famous not because of their specific acts during the American Revolution, but because they happened to live longer than their fellow soldiers. They had nothing in common besides longevity. Their exceptionally long lifespans were rare but not at all unknown during their era; although the average life expectancy in the eighteenth and nineteenth centuries was considerably shorter than in the twenty-first, the longest possible lifespan was not. Statistical averages for lifespan are skewed by the much higher rate of infant and child mortality, giving the impression that long lifespans were unknown. In fact, those who survived into adulthood had a reasonably good chance of reaching sixty or seventy years of age. Only a few became centenarians, but it was not unheard of. Just as today, people wondered what gifts these aged individuals possessed that afforded their long lives, and just as today causality was elusive. The Moore brothers submitted an advanced copy of *The Last Men of the Revolution* to a physician who responded with a letter commenting on the mysteries of remarkable longevity, providing information that only makes it clear how little the phenomenon was understood.[26]

26. The full text of the letter is included in Hillard's book; the writer's name is not given, and although he gives descriptive information about the pensioners there is no evidence that he actually met them. The letter reads as follows:

"Dear Sirs: I thank you for the opportunity of reading the very interesting account of these old patriots 'who have come down to us from a former generation.' From before the first war of Revolution, their lives have extended to the greater second Revolution. Beginning life more than a century ago, with hundreds of thousands of their fellows, in their ascending path to the period of manhood, they saw more than half of their number fall out by the way from disease or accidents; during the most active period and before they came to the down-hill side of life, their ranks became thinner by swift degrees, until having passed beyond the usual extent of life's march, they are come out a solitary few!

"Observations made in vital statistics within the last fifty years, with reference to life insurance, have reduced to a degree of accuracy the probabilities of life for any given age, up to three score and ten; but how many of a population will live beyond a hundred years? A leader of myriads might well weep to engage in the calculation! The number is so few that larger tables are necessary than any that have been compiled, in order to approach any accurate result. The number varies

The last surviving veterans may not have been the longest lived.
There may have been other veterans of the American Revolution
who lived more years than any of the last survivors, but died soon-
er because they were older during the war. An 1842 census of pensioners identified William Prigen living in Bladen County, North

in different countries, and also in different portions of the same country. A rural
population, that lives with sufficient necessaries and few luxuries of life, contented
and laborious in the open air, shows the largest number of centenarians. In the
state of Connecticut, during the year 1863, there were four deaths of those over a
hundred years old,–two males and two females. During the year 1828, there were
in France one hundred and twenty-eight persons who had attained their hundredth year–this in a population of about thirty millions.

"It is known that there are more female centenarians than male.

"What influences have conduced to such long lives? These six old patriots
were of different temperaments, of different stature, and have pursued very different vocations, without much resemblance in their habits of life. Mr. Waldo and
Mr. Cook were large and vigorous. Mr. Link is short and stout, with all the good
and bad tendencies of the sanguine temperament. Mr. Downing is small, with the
nervous temperament predominating; while Mr. Milliner is quite small, not half as
large as Mr. Cook, and not vigorous.

"They have not been alike careful of their health. Mr. Waldo was prudent in
regard to food, and faithfully avoided all excesses; while Mr. Link has lived without any rule or restraint. The others have not been abstemious overmuch, nor yet
has either one been intemperate.

"A sprightly Frenchman has said, that to prolong life it is necessary to have a
bad heart and a good stomach. The latter quality is essential; by the former he
meant, a disposition not easily moved, not enthusiastic. He is so far right; and a
temperament not of the susceptible sort is the most favorable to long life. Such
was the case with Mr. Waldo particularly. But, as if to confound a rule which
seems obviously so correct, the case of Mr. Downing is quite opposite. He is of
the nervous temperament. He is easily and strongly moved by all exciting subjects,
and so has been through life.

"These venerable men seem to agree in several particulars. They have all led
industrious, useful lives, and were active in the use of their limbs. They have been
cheerful, genial, good-humored, and withal blessed with good stomachs. A good
intellectual condition has accompanied them to the end, and is as remarkable as
the persistence of their physical powers. Those who have died seemed not to
have had a long period of dotage, which is so common in those growing old. The
good use of the mind is favorable to the health of the body. Idiots and insane people are not long lived. Among those who have devoted their lives to science and
literature, longevity is notoriously common. It is unnecessary to mention well
known names: the fact is well established.

Carolina, who at 112 was the oldest pensioner alive at that time.[27] A British soldier named Henry Church deserted from his regiment and settled in what became West Virginia where he lived to be just shy of 110 years old.[28] Having been born in 1750, however, he expired four years before the last American pensioners came to public attention. The war's last survivors were born at the right time to be old enough to serve in the war—in some cases just barely—yet young enough to outlive their peers.

Rev. Hillard's book has achieved enduring popularity in spite of falling short in almost every aspect of its intent. The men depicted are not the first, last, or only Revolutionary War veterans photographed; none was the last surviving pensioner nor last surviving soldier; the information about the men and their service records is incomplete and inaccurate. The fact that none of this matters shows the power of visual records. The photographs contained in *The Last Men of the Revolution* are gripping; they hold viewers in a way that no other memorabilia from the war does. The images are static, colorless, and two-dimensional, and yet they vividly represent life, they inspire the imagination, they provoke respect and admiration for their subjects. Simply knowing that these men participated in the great conflict that was the American Revolution makes them heroes in the eyes of anyone who beholds their

"A certain serenity and contentment of mind is noticeable in these old men. They have not been a prey to the corroding passions: the well-timed pensions from the government, for which they took up arms in their younger days, have removed the cares and anxieties for their temporal concerns, which often harass the aged. A firm, calm, religious belief, and a confiding hope in the future, have added beauty as well as strength to their latest years. So we see, that the life which is happiest and best here, has the earnest of that life which is eternal."

27. *Baltimore Sun*, August 25, 1842; the same information was reported in a number of newspapers. The date of Prigen's death is not known.

28. Don N. Hagist, "American Towns Named for British Soldiers," *Journal of the American Revolution*, September 4, 2013, allthingsliberty.com/2013/09/american-towns-named-british-soldiers/.

images. Their specific service doesn't seem to matter; it is the very fact that they were in the army when the war was in progress that makes them great soldiers from a great trial of arms.

The six men in this book are among the most famous common soldiers of the American Revolution, some of the very few whose names are remembered at all. While each one completed the military service required of him, none performed any particular acts to distinguish him from his fellow soldiers; they served honorably but not exceptionally. After the war they lived, for the most part, a routine and humble existence, lives that were normal enough for their era and not remarkable among their peers. It was their longevity, not their deeds, that brought them fame and made them heroes. This, though, is sufficient. All soldiers who become heroes are quick to say that they simply happened to be in the right place at the right time, and did their duty. Chance has always played a great role in this sort of greatness. Living their lives dutifully and well enough to let the chance of longevity keep them alive is heroic enough to warrant the admiration to which all aged veterans are entitled. In their last years, these six men gave hope to a nation by providing a living connection to the past. Through their lasting images, they continue to inspire.

Acknowledgments

THIS BOOK IS THE BRAINCHILD OF BRUCE H. FRANKLIN OF Westholme Publishing and Joseph G. Peterson, who saw the importance of discovering the real stories of the six men profiled in *The Last Men of the Revolution*. Invaluable information on various aspects of the veterans' stories was provided by Bob Allegretto, J. L. Bell, Norm Bollen, Todd W. Braisted, Bob Brooks, Burr Cook (a descendant of Lemuel Cook), Brian Mack of the Fort Plain Museum, John U. Rees, Maureen Taylor, Thomas Verenna, Philip D. Weaver, and the staff of the National Archives. The six original drawings were created by Eric H. Schnitzer. The full-page images of the men and their homes are from an original copy of *The Last Men of the Revolution* owned by The Society of the Cincinnati, and their use here was made possible by Ellen Clark of that institution. Other images of several of the men were made available by Brian Mack, Allan Janus, Burr Cook, Earle Shettleworth, and the staff of the William L. Clements Library.

Index